The INCREDIBLE GRAND CANYON

THE INCREDIBLE GRAND CANYON

STORIES
HISTORY
&
FUN
FACTS

BY

SCOTT THYBONY

Grand
Canyon
Association

Grand Canyon Association

P.O. Box 399
Grand Canyon, AZ 86023-0399
(800)858-2808
www.grandcanyon.org

Edited by Pam Frazier and Todd Berger
Interior Designed by Amanda Summers
Cover Designed by David Jenney Design

Printed in the United States of America

First Edition

17   16   15   14   3   4   5   6

Front Cover Photo: Cline Library Special Collections and Archives, NAU.PH.568.3910
Back Cover Photos: Grand Canyon National Park's Museum Collection

Library of Congress Cataloging-in-Publication Data

Thybony, Scott.
    The incredible Grand Canyon : cliffhangers and curiosities from America's
greatest canyon / by Scott Thybony. -- 1st ed.
        p. cm.
    Includes index.
    ISBN-13: 978-0-938216-94-0 (alk. paper)
    ISBN-10: 0-938216-94-5 (alk. paper)
  1. Grand Canyon (Ariz.)--History--Anecdotes. 2. Grand Canyon National
Park (Ariz.)--History--Anecdotes. I. Title.
    F788.T525 2007
    979.1'32--dc22
                            2007034933

*It is the mission of the Grand Canyon Association to cultivate knowledge,
discovery, and stewardship for the benefit of Grand Canyon National Park
and its visitors. Proceeds from the sale of this book will be used to support
the educational goals of Grand Canyon National Park.*

ACKNOWLEDGEMENTS

A book like this doesn't happen without tapping into a pool of assorted canyon junkies, hardcore hikers, a few stray historians, and a community of rangers, field scientists, and river guides. The cañonistas. Some have already headed downriver; most are still paddling against the stream. My thanks to:

Mary Aiken, John Azar, Kim Besom, Eli Butler, Robert Blake, Martha Blue, Nancy Brian, Terry Brian, Harvey Butchart, Pam Cox, Eric Christensen, Brad Dimock, Dave Edwards, Bob Euler, K.J. Glover, Kenton Grua, Mike Harrison, Colleen Hyde, Martha Krueger, Verlen Kruger, Sjors Hortsman, Steve Landick, Wes Larsen, Chuck LaRue, Jim Mead, Tom Myers, Jim Ohlman, Bob Packard, Mike Quinn, Susan Rogers, George Steck, Larry Stevens, Warren Tracy, Bil Vandergraff, Tony Williams, Dave Wilson, and Bryan Wisher. And special thanks to the publishing team at Grand Canyon Association: Pam Frazier, Todd Berger, Ron Short, and Helen Thompson.

The illustrations in this book were drawn from myriad sources, but two collections proved particularly rich in width and depth: Grand Canyon National Park's Museum Collection (abbreviated as GCNP Museum Collection in credits) and the Cline Library Special Collections and Archives (abbreviated as Cline Library SCA) at Northern Arizona University in Flagstaff. To learn more about these collections visit their Web sites at www.nps.gov/grca/photosmultimedia/index.htm and www.nau.edu/~cline/speccoll/, respectively.

Image identification numbers from these two collections are noted on page 126.

TABLE OF CONTENTS

Introduction: Threshold *9*

First Encounters *12*

Cliffhangers *27*

Nick of Time *38*

The Curious Canyon *44*

Phantom Romance *60*

Onward and Downward: Canyon Guides *64*

Creatures Wild and Tame *70*

Stung, Bit, Chewed *80*

Crazy Weather *84*

Schemes and Grand Dreams *90*

Legends and Mysteries *100*

Grand Canyon by the Numbers *108*

Index *121*

THRESHOLD

FRED HIRSCHMANN

"Yes, yes, yes!" said John Hance, striding down a trail into the Grand Canyon. Few have put it as simply as the canyon's first guide did more than a century ago. Following his lead, this book uses a pared-down approach. It's a light take on the hard facts. Grab it and go.

It includes bits of canyon lore that have slipped through the cracks and a few of the classic stories that still resonate. The people who appear in it range from eminent explorers to canyon characters—both certifiable and aspiring. It includes the best of the tall tales trimmed down to size, the telling facts, a few scandals, a little romance, and some grand schemes gone awry. And since people never seem to tire of hearing about other people getting in over their heads, you'll find a few cliffhangers thrown in.

For years I've guided people below the rims and down the Colorado River. In turn, their enthusiasm for the canyon and its oral traditions has guided me in the selection of these stories. What turns

9

A river trip through the Grand Canyon has been described as offering "hours of quiet contemplation punctuated by moments of sheer terror." LEON WERDINGER

up on these pages amounts to a guide's Cliff Notes, so to speak.

The stories come from people who have lived them: the canyon hiker I've run into days from the nearest trailhead and the wave-battered boatman pulled in below Lava Falls. They come from chance encounters with enthusiastic visitors at Bright Angel Point or beneath the stuffed moose in the lobby of El Tovar. When you're

curious about the lives of others, the world opens in unexpected ways. And a lot of material turns up by simply following leads in an archive the way I might explore a branching canyon on foot.

At first glance the Grand Canyon opens wide before you, exposing everything to view. Nothing is hidden, or so it seems. But the more time spent within it, the more layers you find to peel back—new discoveries, old stories resurfacing, new angles on a familiar landscape. And sometimes you have to work for those new perspectives.

Consider what photographers face each time they get a new assignment to shoot some aspect of the Grand Canyon. So many millions of photographs have been taken of this place, how could they come up with a fresh image? Yet the best of them pull it off time and again.

Bruce Dale sat on the bow of a wooden dory as it ran through Horn Creek Rapid. The *National Geographic* photographer wanted to get a shot of the boatman working the oars in a chaos of crashing waves. What he didn't count on was the tremendous force of the water. The boat hit hard, catapulting him upward. "I kept shooting pictures all the while," he said, "and ran out of film as I was flying through the air."

That's one way to see the canyon; the following pages uncover a few more.

First ENCOUNTERS

Seeing the Grand Canyon for the first time came as a surprise to me. I laughed, because what I encountered was so totally different than the postcard images I had seen. Others cry, and reactions can swing from one extreme to the next. In 1910 George Collingwood, a young forest ranger, traveled with friends to the South Rim. "All we could do was to look," he wrote home, "and then we all swore sort of softly, and in between the curses we would speak of the wonders of God."

The element of surprise produces the greatest impact. Jack Fuss teamed up with a Cherokee named Blair to go trapping in Utah during the winter of 1918–19. They rode north on horseback for a couple of days without knowing where they were, when suddenly they found themselves on the brink of the Grand Canyon.

"We came right out of the cedars," he recalled, "and there it was, kaplunk. I liked to have a heart attack when I thought, 'Am I gonna cross *that* thing?' . . . It scairt me so, I said my prayers right there on the rim. It was so beautiful it took my breath away. I was speechless. I thought, 'Holy smokes, what a show!' It was *magnificent*."

But not everyone gets stopped in their tracks. The canyon can only draw out what you bring to it. Behind the Bright Angel Lodge, a woman walked briskly to the edge, followed by a man with a resigned slump to his shoulders. She took one glance at the canyon and made an abrupt about-face. "You brought me all the way across the country for this?" she asked.

Spanish explorers encountered the Grand Canyon in 1540.   GRAND CANYON ASSOCIATION

FIRST EUROPEANS TO VIEW THE GRAND CANYON

The discovery of the Grand Canyon reads like a page from a child's storybook. Conquistadors led by García López de Cárdenas rode under the desert sun accompanied by friars in black robes and brightly feathered Indians from the Aztec empire. They were searching for seven cities of gold in unknown lands from Hopi country to the Great Plains. The expedition's leader, Francisco Vásquez de Coronado, dispatched an exploring party of a dozen men to find a great river to the west rumored to run through a land of giants. In 1540 anything seemed possible.

After days of hard travel, including a summer crossing of the Painted Desert, a scouting party under Cárdenas reached the brink of a great chasm. Any words uttered by the first Europeans to see the Grand Canyon went unrecorded. It's probably just as well.

The Spanish were hundreds of miles from their frontier outposts, chronically short on water, and forced to trust Hopi guides they had recently defeated in battle. Knowing the Grand Canyon well, the Hopis chose to lead the Spanish explorers to a waterless stretch along the rim, tantalizingly close to a river they could not reach. The Hopis later called this tactic "cooperation without submission." Others might call it payback.

FIRST EUROPEANS TO BITE OFF MORE THAN THEY COULD CHEW

When Spanish explorers led by Cárdenas encountered the Grand Canyon, they set the style for a certain type of visitor who followed. The explorers first wandered around disoriented, ran short on water, ignored the advice of their guides, and then tried hiking to the river and back in one day.

Cárdenas and his men spent three days searching for a practical way to the river, probably in the vicinity of Desert View. When their efforts failed, he sent three men to climb down. They returned late in the day exhausted, having made it only a third of the way to the bottom. Finding no cities of gold and an inaccessible river, the Spanish lost interest in the canyon country for more than two hundred years.

FIRST TO VISIT HAVASU

In 1776 the Franciscan friar Father Francisco Garcés and his guides descended into Havasu Canyon on his way to the Hopi mesas. He became the first European to visit the Havasupai people. Although he found them friendly and hospitable, he was glad to leave behind the "calaboose of cliffs and canyons." He pressed on to the Hopi villages and received a chilly reception. Having a long and bitter history with the Spanish, these pueblo dwellers chased him away.

Two hundred years after Garcés, my wife and I retraced his route to the Hopi country with a couple of friends. What did we learn? After crossing 120 miles (190 km) on foot, we understood why he rode a horse.

MOUNTAIN MEN IN CANYON COUNTRY

A party of fur trappers traveled along the rim of the Grand Canyon in 1826, unsuccessfully searching for good beaver country. One of the disappointed mountain men was James Ohio Pattie, who called the canyons "horrid mountains that caged up the Colorado River and made it useless." Another group of trappers

Father Garcés

under George C. Yount entered the lower gorge, probably through Spencer Canyon, and reached the Colorado River. "The stream descends with a rapidity of current almost unparalleled," he wrote. "At a sudden bend in the channel, the water strikes the rock and flies up in a perpendicular direction more than fifteen yards in one entire foam."

FIRST TO CIRCLE GRAND CANYON

A Mormon exploring party led by Jacob Hamblin left southern Utah in November 1862 to find a new route to the Hopi villages. When they returned fifty-one days later, Hamblin and his men had ridden completely around the Grand Canyon, becoming the first to circle the great chasm. The trip began with a warning from Mormon leader Brigham Young to "Keep your guns as handy as your Bibles."

Twenty-five men crossed the Colorado River near the Grand Wash Cliffs and circled south of the main canyon. Deserted by their Paiute Indian guide and unable to find water, the Mormons were in trouble. Eight horses died of thirst before a snowstorm saved the rest. Hamblin lost another horse in the quicksand pits of the Little Colorado River. A month after leaving their homes, the company approached the first Hopi village, where several hundred armed men appeared along the mesa top. The Hopis had mistaken them for a Navajo war party, but welcomed the Mormons to their homes after learning of their peaceful intentions.

A few days later, Hamblin and his men began the return journey, accompanied by four Hopis. They crossed rough country that looked as if it had been "rolled up edge ways," and lost the trail in deep snow. Finally, the company descended bare slickrock slopes to a river crossing some miles above today's Lees Ferry. The Hopis were reluctant to ford the swift water until they had placed prayer sticks on the river's edge to protect them from drowning.

The river was not the only danger the company faced. Food had run low, forcing the men to subsist on quarter rations. One hungry scout shot a turkey vulture and ate it with relish, licking the pot afterward. The returning party climbed the Kaibab Plateau, trudging through deep snows and hacking out a trail with their butcher knives on the steeper slopes. Half-starved and worn out, they returned to the Mormon settlements in January 1863.

"My horse staggers as he walks," reported John Steele, who was forced to cover the last eight miles (13 km) on foot. Hamblin and his men rejoined their families, thankful the long journey had ended.

A KILLER VIEW

A sightseeing party walked to Lookout Point in 1891 for their first glimpse of the canyon. "The Duchess," said travel writer Charles Dudley Warner, "threw up her arms and screamed." He soon joined her at the rim. "It was a shock so novel," he noted, "that the mind, dazed, quite failed to comprehend it."

During his career as a canyon guide, W. W. Bass had plenty of chances to witness visitor reactions. It was impossible to prepare for the experience, he believed, and he compared the first view to "the flash of forked lightning." His own abrupt encounter came in 1883 while chasing wild cattle at full speed. "It nearly scared me to death," he recalled.

W.W. Bass lectures the Hearst party at the Bass trailhead, 1899.   GCNP MUSEUM COLLECTION

Bass may not have been exaggerating. Six fatalities have been attributed to the visual shock of seeing the canyon. In a moment of vertigo, these victims lost their balance and fell to their deaths. "Ah! the terror of it!" wrote the early travel writer John Van Dyke. "And, worse than that, the mad attraction of it, the dread temptation that lies within! The chasm repels and yet draws."

Each year, two people fall over the edge of the canyon. On average. Of those two, one falls accidentally and the other jumps. Most victims are young males acting recklessly at the time of the accident. Surprisingly, only one child has died from a fall. How many parents have died from heart attacks watching them stray close to the rim hasn't been recorded.

Journalist Irvin S. Cobb noted another phenomenon during a 1913 trip. "Nearly everybody, on taking a first look at the Grand Cañon," he wrote, "comes right out and admits its wonders are absolutely indescribable—and then proceeds to write anywhere from two thousand to fifty thousand words, giving full details."

FIRST NON-NATIVE CANYON RESIDENT

John Hance settled at the South Rim in 1883. On his death in 1919, the old guide also became the first to be buried in the Grand Canyon Cemetery.

FIRST TRAIL GUIDE

John Hance began guiding tourists down canyon trails in 1884. A year earlier, Julius Farlee took tourists by wagon from a railroad stop in Peach Springs to a rustic lodge at the mouth of Diamond Creek in the western canyon, becoming the first tour operator.

FIRST TOURIST

In 1884 John Hance guided the Flagstaff lumberman Edward Ayer down Hance Trail into the canyon. A year later

John Hance is remembered as the Grand Canyon's finest storyteller. He didn't let facts get in the way of a good story.   GCNP MUSEUM COLLECTION (BOTH)

Ayer returned with his wife, Emma, who became the first non-Indian woman to reach the river. Ayer Point is named in her honor.

FIRST POST OFFICE

The first Grand Canyon post office opened near today's Grandview Point with J. H. Tolfree serving as postmaster. When John Hance became postmaster in 1897, he changed the address to "Tourist, Arizona Territory."

FIRST RIM-TO-RIM CROSSING

J. L. Hubbell

The legendary Indian trader Lorenzo Hubbell walked with a limp, the result of having gotten into a scrape as a young man. In 1872 he worked at a Mormon trading post in Kanab, Utah, a staging area that year for a short-lived gold rush drawing hundreds of prospectors into the Grand Canyon.

Few details of the incident are known, but Hubbell admitted having to flee for his life with a bullet in his leg. Rumors say it involved the wife of another man, and in this case, the rumors sound right. Taking in the fugitive, Paiutes treated his wounds until he was able to travel. Hubbell then made his escape by swimming across the Colorado River at the bottom of the canyon. It was a feat, he said, "not many white men have done and lived to tell about."

In 1891 Dan Hogan descended into the gorge from the South Rim, swam the river, and prospected up Bright Angel Canyon to the North Rim. He later built trails, discovered the first copper deposit at what would later become the Orphan Mine, joined the Rough Riders, and was wounded in one of the last armed conflicts with the Navajo.

Louisa Ferrall made a journey from the South Rim to the North in 1906, becoming the first woman to complete a cross-canyon traverse—and she did it without the convenience of a footbridge. With burros in tow, her party crossed the river by boat but the burros broke loose. They had to borrow a couple of horses from trail builder David Rust in order to make it to the North Rim.

FIRST TO HIKE THE LENGTH OF GRAND CANYON

In 1976 Kenton Grua began walking at Lees Ferry and ended his trek thirty-six days later at the Grand Wash Cliffs. He followed the east and south sides of the river. Since the east side is impassable for the first few miles below Lees Ferry, he followed the rim above and entered the gorge at Jackass Canyon. His 1972 attempt to walk it in moccasins failed.

Five years later Bill Ott completed the first traverse of the entire canyon from Lees Ferry to the Grand Wash Cliffs completely below the rim. By using the west and north sides, he was able to piece together a continuous route.

FIRST TO DISCOVER THE HEAD OF NAVIGATION

After running aground Lt. Ives and his crew set out to explore on foot. They found the Grand Canyon to be a formidable obstacle to exploration.   GCNP MUSEUM COLLECTION

In 1857 a military party commanded by Lieutenant Joseph C. Ives steamed up the Colorado River onboard the *Explorer*. Under orders to determine how far upstream a boat could navigate, they made their discovery the hard way. The stern-wheeler entered Black Canyon below the future site of Hoover Dam. Going full tilt it struck a submerged rock, throwing soldiers overboard. With the wheelhouse ripped away and the steam pipe bent double, Ives conceded that he had reached the head of navigation.

Major John Wesley Powell
GCNP MUSEUM COLLECTION

FIRST DESCENT

Major John Wesley Powell was the first to run the Colorado River through the Grand Canyon in 1869; James White was the other first, and the real first was a Hopi called Tiyo.

An expedition led by Major Powell left Green River, Wyoming, on May 24, 1869. Powell had the unsettling habit of singing at the top of his lungs while running dangerous rapids. Fear, madness, or pure exhilaration? A touch of all three, I suspect.

One of the original ten members of the exploring party quit and three others disappeared after leaving the river and climbing out of the gorge. The remnant of the expedition emerged from Grand Canyon ninety-nine days later after floating nearly one thousand miles (1,600 km) and encountering close to five hundred rapids. Powell became a national hero, and his explorations opened one of the last unknown regions of the continental United States.

But was Powell really the first to descend the Colorado? In 1867 an emaciated prospector was rescued from the river clutching the haunch of a dog, which he got from some Paiutes in exchange for a pistol. James White claimed to be the sole survivor of a prospecting party attacked by Ute Indians somewhere above Glen Canyon. White and a companion fled to the river on foot where they built a raft to escape. His companion drowned in a rapid, and fourteen days later, White emerged from the canyon, dazed with hunger and fear. He was unsure of where he had started and remained disoriented throughout his two-week descent. If true, his trip falls into the category of an epic survival rather than an exploration.

When it comes down to it, even White may not be able to claim the first descent. The Hopi tell of a young man, Tiyo, who floated through the Grand Canyon in a hollowed-out cottonwood log. He

Powell's second expedition departed from Green River, WY in 1871. The expedition included photographers E. O. Beaman and John K. Hillers, and crew members Andrew Hattan, Walter C. Powell, Steven V. John, Frederick Dellenbaugh, Almon Thompson, John F. Steward, Francies Bishop, and Frank Richardson.   GCNP MUSEUM COLLECTION

began his journey in Glen Canyon and reached the sea, before returning to his people and introducing the Snake Ceremony.

FIRST GRAND CANYON PROMOTER

To generate publicity for his survey work, Major Powell took Thomas Moran with him to the North Rim in 1873. The artist illustrated Powell's reports, and Congress voted an appropriation of $10,000 to purchase his huge 7-foot by 12-foot (2 x 3.5 m) canvas, *The Chasm of the Colorado*.

Engraving from Powell's report

FIRST DANCE

One evening in 1871, boatmen from John Wesley Powell's second expedition and Mormon scouts gathered around a Navajo campfire at Lees Ferry. Major Powell and his wife Emma were there with Almon Harris Thompson and his wife Nellie. The Navajos had crossed the river with Jacob Hamblin earlier that day and made camp among the willows. Everyone was in a good mood, laughing and talking, when someone asked the Navajos to dance. The Indians agreed on one condition: everyone had to join in.

They built up the fire as the Navajo leader began drumming on an inverted camp kettle. Joining hands, they began dancing "all mixed together," noted Frank Bishop, "singing to us words without meaning, and circling round and round and round, until tired with laughing, hopping, and singing we break the circle shouting so the echoes ring again."

FIRST COMMERCIAL RIVER PASSENGER

In 1909 Julius Stone, a wealthy Ohio investor, got the notion to duplicate Powell's descent of the Green and Colorado rivers. He hired Nathaniel Galloway to build the boats and take him downriver. "He was such a good boatman," Stone wrote, "he could run a boat on a heavy dew." His confidence was not misplaced, and they made a record descent in less than two months.

FIRST TO SWIM THE CANYON

Bill Beer and John Daggett, two California body surfers, decided to make the big swim in the spring of 1955. With minimal gear and no permit, they floated downriver and emerged from the gorge, somewhat waterlogged, twenty-six days later.

Beer and Daggett's swim predated Glen Canyon Dam (1963); they swam an untamed river laden with silt from spring runoff. CLINE LIBRARY SCA (BOTH)

FIRST TO ROW THE RAPIDS BACKWARDS

When Nathaniel Galloway, a Utah trapper, rowed stern-first against the current, he found he had greater control. His pioneering technique has become the standard method for running rapids.

Nathaniel "Than the Man" Galloway's boat in rapid No. 5 in Split Mountain Canyon, 1909. CLINE LIBRARY SCA

23

FIRST WOMEN TO RUN THE RIVER

Botanists Clover and Jotter collected and classified plants along the Colorado River corridor through the canyon.   GCNP MUSEUM COLLECTION

In 1938 Norm Nevills guided the first commercial trip down the Colorado River. Elzada Clover and Lois Jotter, two of his passengers, became the first women to traverse the entire river through the Grand Canyon.

The first woman to attempt running the Colorado was Bessie Hyde. She disappeared on a river trip in 1928 and may have reached as far as Mile 232 Rapid.

FIRST BEAR TO RUN THE RIVER

In 1927 Clyde Eddy took a black bear cub named Cataract downriver as a mascot.

LAST BEAR TO RUN THE RIVER

Cataract. It may have been the last bear to run the river, but a wild bear was spotted along the river bank in spring 2005.

FIRST AUTOMOBILE TO REACH THE SOUTH RIM

Oliver Lippincott sat behind the wheel of the steam-powered Toledo Eight-horse on its pioneering trip to the canyon in 1902.

Lippincott and his Toledo Eight-horse required a horse tow.
GCNP MUSEUM COLLECTION

Convinced it would only take 3½ hours from Flagstaff to the South Rim, he failed to take extra supplies.

Plagued by breakdowns, the party was forced to bivouac in a cowboy cabin, and by morning the motor had frozen. This required burning enough gas to thaw the boilers, a fix which only postponed their troubles. Back on the road, they ran out of fuel eighteen miles (29 km) from the rim and had to get rescued with a horse and wagon. Five days after leaving town, the auto managed to reach its destination. In those days, the stagecoach took twelve hours, and the first bicycle trip in 1894 had taken fourteen hours. Anyone making predictions based on the first automobile trip would have been astonished by their later success. More than a million cars would enter the national park within the next fifty years.

FIRST AUTOMOBILE TO REACH THE NORTH RIM

In 1909 a team headed by Edwin D. Woolley took eighteen days to make a round-trip journey from Salt Lake City to the North Rim. They drove it with two vehicles, a Thomas Flyer and the appropriately-named Locomobile, the latter getting three miles per gallon.

FIRST AIRPLANE TO LAND IN THE CANYON

The first airplane flew over the Grand Canyon in 1919. Three years later a barnstormer named Royal V. Thomas took his biplane into a tailspin as crowds of tourists watched from the rim. Spiraling into the gorge, he pulled out of his dive and landed safely near Plateau Point. More surprisingly, he managed to take off again.

First Airplane Landing made in the Grand Canyon of Arizona on Aug 8. 1922. R.V.Thomas Pilot   E.L.Kolb Passenger-Cameraman

Royal Thomas (left) and Ellsworth Kolb pose at Plateau Point.
GCNP MUSEUM COLLECTION

FIRST MIDAIR COLLISION OVER THE CANYON

Two airliners collided above the confluence of the Colorado and Little Colorado rivers in 1956, killing all 128 passengers and crew. At the time, it was the worst civil aviation disaster in history, and the incident led to the creation of the Federal Aviation Administration.

Memorial at Grand Canyon Cemetery
GCNP MUSEUM COLLECTION

Mooney Falls

FRED HIRSCHMANN

*Cliff*HANGERS

A land of cliffs naturally generates its share of cliffhangers. Some stories, like that of prospector Dan Mooney, end tragically. My favorites are the near misses, the accounts of people who get in over their heads but by grace or grit manage to pull through.

MOONEY'S FALL

In the winter of 1880 Billy Beckman led a prospecting party into Havasu Canyon by way of "one of the roughest trails ever traveled by man"—the standard route in those days. Red-bearded Dan Mooney, a former sailor, packed in a thin rope he planned to use in descending to the pool below the highest waterfall. The Havasupais claimed no one had ever passed beyond the falls. It was only possible, they said, for "birds of the air or spirits of the dead."

Exactly how Mooney fell to his death is uncertain. Havasupai Juan Sinyella said that as the other miners tried to lower him, the rope slipped into a crevice in the rough travertine and jammed. Those above were unable to lower or raise him. As they worked the rope up and down, it quickly frayed and broke, sending Mooney to his death. Years later, an eyewitness account from a fellow prospector gave a somewhat different version.

Alphonso Humphreys told his family Mooney had removed his boots and began climbing down the rope. He disappeared from sight over the cliff edge, and the roar of the falls prevented them from communicating. But they soon realized something had gone wrong. Future oil baron Edward L. Doheny stood watching from above and later remarked that the prospector's death did not come as a complete surprise. "Mooney was very reckless," he said, "and did not exercise the caution that 100 percent sanity would dictate."

Next morning Beckman untied the rope and tossed it into the canyon along with Mooney's boots. "This is all the funeral I can give you this time," he said.

SCARIEST TRAIL

Reporter George Smalley traveled to the South Rim in the summer of 1897 to write about the flurry of mining activity taking place. After the reporter visited the Orphan Mine below Powell Point, miner Dan Hogan suggested he take a shortcut back to the rim—straight up the cliff on the Hummingbird Trail. Known as

Hogan's Slide or the Hummingbird Trail, the route consisted of a series of hand- and toeholds Hogan had cut into the rock face. He had also drilled holes at strategic points, and he handed the reporter a wooden peg. When the strain on his feet became too great, he was instructed to jam the peg in a hole and hang on. "Mr. Smalley in his ascent," wrote another reporter, "was handicapped by a pair of razor-toe shoes."

The Hummingbird Trail was Hogan's shortcut to the rim through the sheer cliffs of Kaibab Limestone and Coconino Sandstone below today's Powell Point.   GCNP MUSEUM COLLECTION

Smalley, the first tenderfoot to attempt the climb, had no idea what he was getting himself into. A single slip, he discovered, meant a thousand-foot (300-m) fall. He survived the hair-raising climb, and in a classic understatement wrote, "It was a real adventure, but one I would not care to repeat."

RIDING OUT THE STORM

Canyon photographers Emery and Ellsworth Kolb descended from the North Rim in 1930 to explore the cave behind Cheyava Falls. Fed by snowmelt in the spring, the waterfall plunged eight hundred feet (250 m) in a series of cascades, but slowed to a wet streak on the wall at other times of the year.

To reach the cliff above the falls, the brothers were forced to bivouac two nights in the open. They descended one eighty-foot (24-m) cliff by snagging the top of a tall fir twenty feet (6 m) away with a rope, climbing across it and then down the tree. On top of the Redwall cliff above the falls, they began rigging a boom with a block-and-tackle attached. It was evening by the time they finished. But since they had run out of water, Ellsworth insisted on making the two-hundred-foot (60-m) descent to the cave opening. Clear Creek flowed one thousand feet (300 m) below them, and storm clouds were gathering over-head. Taking the canteen, Ellsworth sat in a loop of rope as his brother slowly lowered him. Halfway down, the storm broke loose. The brothers were caught in what Emery described as "one of the most terrific rain and hail storms I have ever witnessed."

Lightning struck all around, and a fierce wind nearly blew Emery off the cliff. Forced to take shelter, he tied the rope off and left his brother dangling in midair. The winds whipped about, spinning Ellsworth

The Kolb brothers explored and photographed remote parts of the canyon.
GCNP MUSEUM COLLECTION

around until the ropes were hopelessly tangled. He was stuck hanging over a sheer drop in the middle of a wild thunderstorm. Once the storm eased, Ellsworth slowly unwound himself, and Emery continued lowering him to the cave mouth. Ellsworth filled the canteen and was pulled up the cliff face to the top, utterly exhausted.

UNDERGROUND FLOOD

Four cave explorers climbed into Falls Cave, high on a cliff face at Vaseys Paradise, in late January 1969. After a run of stormy weather, the sky above Marble Canyon that morning was clear. All were experienced spelunkers, except Jon Howe, who was on his first caving trip. And all were about to be caught in a frightening turn of events.

Entering the cave, they followed a shallow stream as they pushed deep through the underground passageway. Nine hours later the cavers turned back. Only when they were within eight hundred feet (245 m) of the entrance did they realize something was wrong. To their surprise, what had been an ankle-deep stream was now waist-deep. An underground flood had filled the passageway, and the water was continuing to rise. They feared the entrance might soon be blocked, trapping them inside the cave.

Pushing on, they reached a section flooded eight feet (2.4 m) deep, and for the last 170 feet (52 m) had to swim. Close to the entrance, only five inches (13 cm) of air space remained, forcing them to remove their helmets. They swam through the last passage with water lapping at their chins. "I made it out scraping my carbide lamp against the ceiling," Robert Blake told me. "I was the only one able to keep it lit."

A perennial spring at the base of the Redwall Limestone creates a lush oasis at Vaseys Paradise, river mile 31.5.
JOSEF MUENCH COLLECTION, CLINE LIBRARY SCA

At 3:00 AM they left the cave after having spent fifteen hours underground. Soaking wet, Jerry Hassemer rigged the rappel in subfreezing temperatures with a stiff wind blowing. They kept moving to keep warm. Several hours after reaching their camp below, they watched as water gushed from the entrance in a dramatic waterfall. If anything had delayed them, they would have been trapped. At best. "We had made it safely," Al Williams reported, "but it had been too close a call."

Falls Cave has at least two miles (3 km) of passages, but exploration of it has ceased. Caves within the national park are off-limits without a special permit that is rarely granted.

SURPRISE BLIZZARD

In November 1981 Bob Packard and Ken Walters set out to climb eleven buttes below the North Rim. Both were instructors at Northern Arizona University and had nine days to spend in the national park before classes resumed. They descended the Nankoweap Trail and worked their way south, climbing as they went.

All was going well until a cold front moved in one night, freezing the water in their canteens. They didn't carry a tent, which is not unusual on canyon hikes. The next day it began to snow and the wind blew without letting up. Surprised by the intensity of the late-fall storm, the two climbers ascended Lava Creek on their planned route back to the rim. More snow fell that night. The next day they attempted to climb Hubbell Butte in a blizzard, but were forced to back off. "Now," Packard told me, "we knew we were in a life or death situation."

Clouds covered the canyon rim to rim. The route out was difficult even in perfect conditions, but the severe weather heightened the danger. That night they bivouacked below Atoka Point, and Packard's feet became frostbitten. "It's a strange, strange feeling," he said. "Yes, they felt cold, but the main thing is they felt wooden." At daybreak they continued to the rim, struggling to push through the deep snow. "It was a supreme effort," he said. "It took tremendous energy to come out—enormous energy."

When they reached the plateau, two feet (60 cm) of snow covered the Cape Royal Road, closed for the winter. For two days they post-holed through crusted drifts as temperatures dropped below zero at night. Each morning their boots, frozen solid, had to be thawed by heating water from melted snow, pouring it into water bottles, and forcing the bottles into the boots. During the day they pressed on, following the rim back to where they had left their truck at Saddle Mountain. By the time they reached it, eleven days after entering the canyon, they were out of food, out of water, and out of fuel.

"What kept you going?" I asked Packard.

Snowfall on the North Rim (in distance) can exceed 250 inches.

"If we stopped," he said, "it was death."

Walters soon recovered from the ordeal, but Packard spent 3½ weeks in the hospital being treated for frostbite. Healing took several months, and while the doctor was able to save Packard's toes, several were permanently damaged.

BENSON'S CRAWL

To make his mark, Robert Benson Eschka wanted to do something no one had ever done before. A German citizen, he took the name Robert Benson from a gravestone when his visa expired, and most knew him by that name. Benson finally settled on becoming the first person to hike the length of the Grand Canyon on both sides of the river—and he threw in Cataract Canyon and other parts of Canyonlands National Park and Glen Canyon to boot. During his downriver trek in 1982 he nearly died.

Historic ranger cabin on Muav Saddle (left) and after a 1995 restoration.

Climbing alone, Benson was descending Elaine's Castle below the North Rim when he took a thirty-foot (9 m) fall. He landed hard and lost consciousness, and when he came to, he was unable to move. For the next half hour he had time to contemplate his own death. As the shock paralysis wore off, the pain kicked in.

Alone in a remote corner of Grand Canyon and unable to walk, Benson began to crawl. He crawled for the next five days in extreme pain, dragging his pack behind him. He followed a rocky, cactus-choked route above Shinumo Creek and eventually intersected the North Bass Trail. Although one of the roughest trails in the canyon, it felt like a superhighway. He pulled himself up the steep trail and reached an old ranger cabin in Muav Saddle. "Very tired," Benson wrote in his diary, "but couldn't sleep, in pain all night."

While he was convalescing at the cabin, a ranger appeared on the scene and offered to take him to the hospital. The trip meant too much to him, so Benson refused to be evacuated. He had to go on. After hiking for 144 days, he reached the end of the Grand Canyon and completed the first stage of his momentous trek. Only then did he learn he had broken his pelvis and fractured several vertebrae.

Benson returned to New Mexico and recuperated for a few

months before returning to the canyon. This time he pieced together routes on the south side of the Colorado River, taking five months to trek upriver to reach Moab, Utah.

AGAINST THE FLOW

On April Fools' Day 1983, Verlen Kruger and Steve Landick approached the lower end of Grand Canyon after having paddled upriver from the Sea of Cortez. Three years earlier, they had set out on an epic twenty-eight-thousand-mile (45,000-km) exploration of North America by canoe.

The route they took maps the geography of an entire continent. They launched at the headwaters of the Missouri River, crossed the Great Lakes, and skirted the Atlantic coast. Paddling against spring runoff, they ascended the Mississippi River and then descended the Mackenzie to the Arctic Ocean, racing against freeze-up. To reach the Pacific Ocean, they had to portage over the infamous Chilkoot Pass. They then followed the coast of California, and, after rounding Baja, ascended the Colorado River. The two canoeists now faced the greatest challenge of their entire journey.

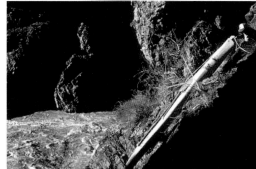

Grand Canyon's notorious whitewater and sheer cliffs forced Kruger and Landick to make 200 portages.
PHOTOS COURTESY OF STEVE LANDICK

"Steve and I didn't let what looked impossible stop us," Kruger told me. "We were going to make it one way or the other. We had come a long ways, and nothing was going to stop us. It was just a question of how we were going to do it." He was sixty-one years old at the time and Landick was half his age.

For three weeks in April they maneuvered upriver through the Grand Canyon, making two hundred portages. Each portage took two carries—the first to haul packs weighing up to one hundred pounds (45 kg) and the next carrying the two sixty-pound (27-kg) canoes. At one unnamed rapid, they were forced to make a night portage, traversing a cliff face high above the river. Kruger and

Paddling upstream through the Grand Canyon proved to be the greatest challenge of Kruger and Landick's 28,000-mile journey.

Landick tied themselves together and passed a single flashlight, held in the mouth, back and forth to find handholds.

When they reached the foot of Sockdolager Rapid, the entire expedition hung in the balance. "It was the focal point of the whole trip," Landick said. "During the three years before, people who looked at the map of our route would see the Grand Canyon and say, 'How are you going to do that?' And we couldn't really say, other than we figured we could do it. And it was that rapid in the Grand Canyon that held the key. Looking up at the flat water above Sockdolager Rapid was like looking at the Promised Land."

At first it looked impossible with sheer cliffs rising straight from the river on both sides. Kruger and Landick scouted a portage on river left and found a sketchy route. "We were 150 vertical feet off the water," Landick said, "and there were places where you could fall a ways." The rapids thundered below them; one slip and it would be all over.

"It was tough," Kruger recalled. "We had one final piece of sheer wall that we had to get around. We took all the rope that we had, put half of it on the front end and half on the stern. I went around and started pulling on the canoe and Steve started letting out the rope. There was a little bit of a ledge for a little ways, then the ledge ran out and there was nothing but sheer wall. We had the canoe hanging in space with only each other to keep it up. And before it got to me, Steve ran out of rope." He laughed at their predicament. "So I dug in my heels as best I possibly could, leaned back, and hollered for him to let it go. The canoe swung down, ka-wombitty-woomp." He paused a moment and then added, "I managed to hang on."

They completed the treacherous portage and continued upriver, entering Marble Canyon. When they were fourteen miles (23 km) below Lees Ferry, they encountered another barrier. "Sheer Wall Rapid looked like it was going to stop us," Kruger said. "It looked like we were going to have to go downstream and find a canyon, climb out, and then hike along the top and climb back down in some place. But we tackled it straight on."

Twice they had to ferry across standing waves and the powerful, surging current. Landick used his double-bladed paddle to grab the wall and pull himself upriver, but Kruger had a regular canoe paddle without as much reach. Finally, his partner passed him a line, and they soon got above the rapid. It was the toughest paddling they had faced in the entire canyon.

Reaching Lees Ferry, the paddlers were elated. They had overcome the greatest obstacle on the continent, and they knew nothing could stop them now. And that December, 3½ years after Kruger and Landick set out, and 24 million paddle strokes later, they ended the journey at Lansing, Michigan. Their expedition has never been matched.

As he was wrapping up his account, Kruger mentioned something about not being able to swim worth beans. Uncertain if I'd heard him right, I asked, "You covered 28,000 miles in a canoe and you can't swim?"

"It makes you a better paddler," he said with a laugh.

Landick (left) and Kruger at Lees Ferry
PHOTO COURTESY OF STEVE LANDICK

GREATEST SHEER DROP

The most extreme drop reachable by car lies at the end of a sixty-one-mile (98-km) dirt road in the western Grand Canyon. At Toroweap Overlook, visitors can look over what appears to be a straight drop from the rim to the river almost three thousand feet

Twist OF FATE

A doctor informed an ailing W. W. Bass that he might be able to live a few more months if he left New York City for a different climate. Bass took the doctor's advice and arrived in Arizona when he was thirty-four years old. But instead of succumbing to his illness, he went on to father four children, build fifty-five miles (89 km) of canyon trail, file claims on twenty mining and mill sites, build two stagecoach roads to the rim, and live to be eighty-four years old. That proved long enough for him to return to the city and put flowers on the grave of his doctor.

Bass used his influence with the Havasupai people to help bring an end to their custom of cremating the dead. But he didn't practice what he preached. Upon his death in 1933, the canyon guide's own remains were cremated and his ashes scattered by airplane over Holy Grail Temple.

(910 m) below. But Tony Williams tells me the longest free drop is 703 feet (214 m), and since he rappelled it, I'll let his figures stand. His party rigged a continuous rope, 4,600-feet (1,400-m) long, using 4,300 feet (1,310 m) of it to reach from the rim to the river down a series of sheer drops, ledges, and slopes.

FATEFUL LAST WORDS

O'Neill Butte on the South Kaibab Trail was named for Buckey O'Neill. He chased down train robbers as a sheriff, edited a frontier newspaper, prospected in the Grand Canyon during the 1890s, and was a key promoter of a railroad to the South Rim. At the outbreak of the Spanish-American War, he raised a company of Rough Riders only to be killed in action leading them into battle. To set an example of bravery for his men, he had refused to take cover when they came under heavy fire. He died instantly with a shot to the head after having tempted fate by saying, "The Spanish haven't made the bullet that will get me."

INVENTION AS THE MOTHER OF NECESSITY

In the 1930s Marvin Gandy designed a mule-mounted litter to carry an injured person out of the canyon. He became the first victim to use his invention after an attack of appendicitis forced him to be evacuated to the hospital.

THE CALL OF THE CANYON

Grand Canyon has a way of changing people's lives. When a friend of river guide Roger Henderson took his first down the Colorado, there was trip no turning back. "He knew this was it," Henderson said. "This was what he wanted to do with his life." His friend was married at the time and working for an oil company out of Calgary. After the boats reached Phantom Ranch, he sent two postcards stamped, "Mailed by Mule at the Bottom of the Grand Canyon."

"One," Henderson said, "went to his wife, telling her he wanted a divorce. The other went to his boss saying, 'I quit.'"

GCNP MUSEUM COLLECTION

MAILED BY MULE AT THE BOTTOM OF THE GRAND CANYON PHANTOM RANCH

"The Grand Canyon at the Foot of the Toroweap Looking East" by William H. Holmes from Dutton's *Atlas to Accompany the Monograph on the Tertiary History of the Grand Cañon District* (Washington D. C., 1882).

NICK OF *Time*

The human drama often gets lost in Grand Canyon's immense scale. Life and death situations can play out within sight of thousands of visitors on the rim without anyone noticing. When danger comes, whether a stampeding buffalo or a flash flood, it can happen suddenly. And just as quickly, rescuers go into action to save those in trouble.

<hr/>

INCIDENT AT HELLHOLE BEND

In the spring of 1934 Horace Moulton and two companions took off from Desert View to explore the Little Colorado River Gorge. They carried one hundred feet (30 m) of rope and food for a week, along with a gold pan to do some prospecting. The forty-year-old Moulton worked as a foreman for the Emergency Conservation Works Administration. By late afternoon on Thursday, their first day out, they were down to a quart of water.

The three men decided to take a shortcut to the river, sunk within a sheer-walled canyon 1,500 feet (450 m) below. Finding a promising ravine upstream from Hellhole Bend, they doubled the thin rope around a projecting rock and climbed down the first cliff. A final ninety-foot (27-m) drop blocked the route near the bottom.

Moulton began descending hand-over-hand with the rope looped around his foot as a break. Halfway down his speed increased until the rope burned through the flesh of his hands. Unable to hold on, he fell the last forty feet (12 m) and hit a patch of sand between boulders, probably saving his life. His right leg was fractured and his ankle badly dislocated. "Well, that's it," his friends heard him say.

They climbed back to the rim and went for help. Stranded on a ledge above the river, Moulton suffered through a long, sleepless night. "The pain was terrific," he said. "The bones grated together every time I moved."

A rescue team of twenty Civilian Conservation Corps men, led by Grand Canyon National Park rangers and the victim's two friends, set out early Friday morning. They descended a rough route, probably the Moody Trail, and reached the river on the downstream side of Hellhole Bend. They worked up the boulder-choked gorge and found Moulton by early afternoon. The injured climber was placed in a stretcher, and they continued up the canyon toward Hopi Trail

Crossing, fourteen miles (23 km) away. The old trail crossed the river at the head of the gorge and followed a good route through the outer cliffs.

But the Little Colorado River was rising fast. Thunder boomed between the cliff walls and lightning flashed in the distance. By nightfall, the men were in water up to their armpits. The exhausted team bivouacked high above the river in case of a flash flood, and early Saturday morning they pushed on.

Cliffs blocked their way, forcing them to ford the river dozens of times. At each crossing, six of them hoisted the stretcher above their heads with others helping to steady it. The work grew increasingly dangerous as the rescuers hit stretches of quicksand, forcing them to lunge through it or flatten out to prevent sinking deeper. As the gorge narrowed, the current grew almost strong enough to sweep them off their feet. And throughout the ordeal, Moulton continued to suffer intense pain.

Chief Ranger James Brooks hiked in to check the upper crossing and didn't like what he saw. The river was at flood stage, filling the canyon bottom wall to wall. He sent word to the rescue team not to attempt it. Their only hope was a slide three miles (5 km) downstream, probably a precipitous route called the Dam Site Trail. Upon reaching it the rescuers found it was too steep to climb while carrying the victim. So the men formed a line stretching up the broken cliffs and passed the stretcher over their heads.

A pair of twenty-five-foot (8-m) cliffs forced them to take the injured man out of the stretcher and tie a rope under his arms. They hauled from above while he pulled on a second rope, helping the effort but ratcheting up the pain. It took them two hours to raise him only three hundred feet (90 m) above the river to the top of the cliff, but once out of the canyon things moved quickly. By 9:30 that night, Moulton was at the Grand Canyon hospital. Amazed by the stamina of his rescuers, he said, "There was no quit to them."

J.T. Owens.   GCNP MUSEUM COLLECTION

UNCLE JIM TO THE RESCUE

Texas cowboy James T. Owens arrived at the North Rim in 1907, driving a herd of buffalo. Uncle Jim had the reputation of being absolutely fearless. During the summer, he had a cabin in Harvey Meadow and kept his herd of two dozen animals nearby. Each day, the buffalo trailed through the meadow on their way to Bright Angel Spring. Since their actions were unpredictable, Uncle Jim had to be prepared for anything, especially with one he knew to be "right down ornery."

A party of tourists, including two girls, camped near his cabin in 1911. Earlier, Uncle Jim had warned the girls to wait in camp until the herd had safely passed. They followed his instructions and waited, but not long enough. Before the herd was out of sight, the girls entered the meadow, and one of them began to open and close an umbrella. The sudden motion spooked the bison, and they stampeded. With the ornery buffalo taking the lead, the herd thundered to the end of the meadow and abruptly turned back—heading straight for the girls. They ran in separate directions, and the lead buffalo began to overtake the one closest to the cabin. Its head was lowered and its lethal horns pointed forward.

Owens tending the herd that he and C. J. "Buffalo" Jones established on the North Rim in 1907; this photo circa 1920.
GCNP MUSEUM COLLECTION

Uncle Jim took in the situation at a glance and grabbed a stout piece of wood. Giving a Comanche war cry, he ran straight toward the charging buffalo. He reached the animal at the last possible moment and swung with all his might, knocking it square on the nose. The lead buffalo veered away, barely missing the girls, and the herd followed.

LOST AND FOUND

Linda Fortney, a twenty-five-year-old nurse, became disoriented and took a wrong turn on the trail to Supai in 1975. It was her first hike in the Grand Canyon. With a little dog at her side, she wandered ten miles (16 km) up Cataract Canyon. The lost hiker went three days without water, nearly dying of thirst, before finding a small seep. It took forty-five minutes to fill her eyeglass case, but it kept her alive—for nineteen days. Finally, a Havasupai spotted her tracks and found the woman still alive. At the time of her rescue she weighed only eighty-five pounds (39 kg), having dropped twenty-five pounds (11 kg) during the ordeal. Her dog had already found its way out a couple of days earlier.

STRANDED IN A RAPID

A 37-foot-long (11-m-long) motor
raft lined up to run Unkar
Rapid in the summer of
2003. Suddenly, the
motor quit, and the
boat drifted into the
churning white-
water. Near the
bottom of the
rapid, it caught
on the rocks,
and all efforts
to dislodge
it failed. The
boat was stuck
in the rapid,
preventing the
passengers, all
women, from
reaching land. A
distress call placed
by satellite phone
alerted a park service
search-and-rescue team
headed by K. J. Glover. Before dark, they short-hauled six
passengers using a one-hundred-
foot-long (30-m-long) rope slung below

National Park Service search-
and-rescue team executes a
short-haul rescue.
NPS PHOTO BY KEN PHILLIPS

a helicopter. The rest spent the night stranded on the raft. Rescue
operations resumed the next morning, and the remaining eleven
were airlifted to shore without further incident.

THE NIGHT FLOOD

Heavy rains fell onto already saturated ground at Cottonwood
Campground in Bright Angel Canyon during a September night
in 1992. And then the storm intensified. Waterfalls began pouring
over the cliffs in broad sheets, and in an instant Bright Angel Creek
was flashing.

Ranger Bryan Wisher ran to the campground, yelling for everyone to abandon their tents and head for high ground. Some were
too afraid to move. Floodwaters swept over camp as normally dry
washes became sudden torrents, wrapping tents around boulders.

Wisher waded into the flood to assist campers as boulders tumbled along the creekbed and driftwood logs shot past. Spotting a light inside a tent, he pushed through water above his waist to drag the tent and its occupant to safety. Before the night ended, Wisher had saved twenty-eight lives.

BIG WATER

On a single day in 1983, four 37-foot-long (11-m-long) rafts flipped in Crystal Rapid during unusually high water. Two of those boats were destroyed, one passenger died, and the park rangers airlifted ninety-four others to safety. Until the water dropped to safer levels, the National Park Service closed the rapid and required passengers to walk around it.

Motor rig in swift water   LEON WERDINGER

43

Blanche Kolb (Emery's wife) and unidentified visitor (left) at the darkroom at Indian Garden, circa 1910.

THE *Curious* CANYON

Bizarre incidents, strange characters, odd crimes, and improbable events come with the turf at Grand Canyon. In this land of extremes you soon learn to take the unusual for granted.

AEROBIC PHOTOGRAPHY

In the early days, clean water was in short supply on the South Rim, making it difficult to develop photographs. Water had to be hauled up from the springs at Indian Garden in kegs lashed to burros. Pioneer photographer Emery Kolb came up with a solution by moving his darkroom down to the springs. In the morning he took photos of mule riders at the top of the Bright Angel Trail, ran to Indian Garden 4.6 miles (7.2 km) below the rim, developed his exposed film, made the prints, and then ran back to the top in time to deliver the finished pictures to the returning riders. Two round-trips a day were not uncommon, and on one occasion Emery made three trips in a single day.

THE MAN IN THE PIN-STRIPED SUIT

A hiker wearing a pin-striped suit and turban appeared at Phantom Ranch with the intention of hiking to the North Rim. The only problem—it was winter. The ranger told him six feet (1.8 m) of snow blocked the trail ahead and turned him back. The hiker was last seen illegally setting brush on fire to keep warm as he made his way back to the South Rim.

L to R: Astronauts Donald "Deke" Slayton and Jim McDivitt, with geologist Dale Jackson on training trip to Grand Canyon in March 1964.   NASA PHOTO

MOONWALK

On a training exercise in 1964, a group of Apollo astronauts walked down the South Kaibab Trail—without their spacesuits. The next day, not yet ready to take that giant leap for mankind, they returned to the rim on muleback.

MOST IMPROBABLE ITEM PACKED DOWN THE TRAIL

Two professional piano movers, ten Havasupais, and seven horses managed to pack a baby grand piano down the Topocoba Trail to the village of Supai in 1923. First, they disassembled it, but found the largest piece still weighed 378 pounds (171 kg). Since a horse could only carry two hundred pounds (91 kg), they built a crate supported by long poles and attached these to horses front and rear. This worked well on the straight stretches, but at each switchback they had to hand-carry the pieces. Remarkably, the crew completed the fourteen-mile (23-km) trek in eight hours, then reassembled it in time to play a concert that evening. The piano didn't have a scratch.

CRAZIEST ITEM PACKED ACROSS THE CANYON

Charles Jesse "Buffalo" Jones and Uncle Jim Owens used dogs to tree mountain lions on the North Rim. On one occasion they climbed above the cornered animal and slipped a noose over its head. After yanking it out of the tree, they muzzled it and clipped its claws. The lion was carried on the back of a burro to the South Rim, using a cable car to cross the river.

HEAVIEST ITEM CARRIED DOWN THE TRAIL

During construction of the Kaibab Suspension Bridge in 1928, the eight main cables were carried down the South Kaibab Trail on the shoulders of forty-two men, mostly Havasupais. A single cable weighed more than a ton.

MOST IMPROBABLE ITEM HAND-CARRIED DOWN THE TRAIL

In 1936 one hundred men from the Civilian Conservation Corps eagerly volunteered to haul a pool table from the rim to their work camp at the bottom of the canyon along Bright Angel Creek. Fifty chosen men left early Saturday morning, picked up the heavy slate slabs and other pieces of the table at the South Kaibab trailhead at Yaki Point, and returned to camp on Sunday afternoon.

After hauling a bridge cable down the Kaibab Trail, Havasupai men made a sweat bath and then had a footrace back to the rim.

GCNP MUSEUM COLLECTION

Civilian Conservation Corps camp 818 at Phantom Ranch was located where Bright Angel Campground is today.
GCNP MUSEUM COLLECTION

MISSION OF MERCY

A boatman wheeled a hand truck down the trail carrying ten cases of beer to resupply a river trip. Wheels are not allowed on canyon trails. Caught by a ranger, he had to haul his load back to the top with a ticket in his pocket for his troubles.

MOST IMPROBABLE ITEM PACKED UP THE TRAIL

Smithsonian Institution geologist Charles Gilmore used horses to pack out 1,700 pounds (770 kg) of rock slabs containing ancient fossil tracks. Gilmore collected most of these specimens of reptile footprints along the Hermit Trail in the 1920s.

SURPRISING BUT TRUE

Walking downhill is harder than walking on flat ground. A study found that more energy is expended walking downhill than on a flat surface. The body must check its forward momentum, fighting gravity to keep from tumbling head over heels.

The tracks of reptiles crossing sand dunes 275 million years ago are preserved in the Coconino Sandstone. BILL HATCHER

YOU'RE HIKING IN WHAT?

High heels. People have also tried hiking into the canyon wearing everything from flip-flops to wing tips. And, yes, barefoot.

A MOST UNLUCKY PASSENGER

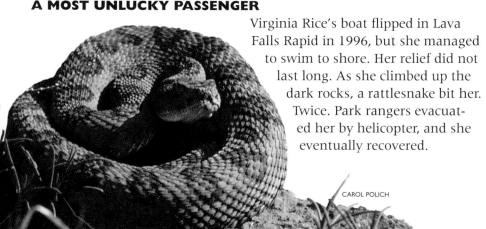

Virginia Rice's boat flipped in Lava Falls Rapid in 1996, but she managed to swim to shore. Her relief did not last long. As she climbed up the dark rocks, a rattlesnake bit her. Twice. Park rangers evacuated her by helicopter, and she eventually recovered.

CAROL POLICH

MOST BIZARRE INNER-CANYON ACCIDENT

After running Lava Falls Rapid, a river party put into camp and a boatman pulled out a golf club. A tamarisk tree hid from view a passenger who was setting up camp. The river guide took a hefty swing and drove the ball one hundred yards (90 m), knocking the passenger in the head. The injuries were judged serious enough to require a helicopter evacuation.

MOST UNUSUAL WAY TO DELIVER MAIL

Mail is regularly delivered on muleback to the village of Supai on the Havasupai Indian Reservation, a mail route in operation since 1896. Mules also carry the mail up from Phantom Ranch. One December I hiked to Phantom with a stack of Christmas cards and had them stamped, "Mailed by Mule at the Bottom of the Grand Canyon." Then I turned around and hiked back. That might explain why I stopped sending Christmas cards.

Supai Village is perhaps the country's most remote address. Mail is delivered by mule to the Havasupai Reservation deep inside the Grand Canyon.   TERRY EILER

WILDEST WHITEWATER RUN

An unusually high flow in the summer of 1983 was flipping boats up and down the river. At what appeared to be an unrunable stage, Georgie White steered her Triple-Rig, with thirty passengers onboard, straight for the tremendous hole in Crystal Rapid. The seventy-two-year-old river runner wore a helmet strapped on her head and her trademark leopard-skin bathing suit.

She shut off the motor, braced herself in a sitting position, and

49

stuck her wrists into a pair of eye-splices. "She's taking it in dead-stick with no power, just drifting," said river ranger Terry Brian, who was watching from shore. She dropped into the hole as waves broke over the bow, and the deep trough of water buried the boat.

Georgie White (below) led low-budget river trips on her infamous Triple-Rig (above), whereby three inflatable boats were lashed together for a wild ride.

GCNP MUSEUM COLLECTION (ABOVE) AND CLINE LIBRARY SCA (BELOW)

"As it climbed out," he continued, "the wave would crash, and the whole raft would buckle. Then it would spring back, and people would pop out. Not only were they catapulted out—they were also catapulted through the boat between the pontoons. It was just crazy. I'm sitting there with my mouth wide open."

And then Brian spotted White crawling out of the motor well. "There was not a stitch of anything else on the boat," he said. "There was nothing, absolutely nothing. Gas cans, old food bags, and all the duffels—just gone. All she had was the fuel in her gas line and her motor, that was it."

She was able to fire up the motor and land above the next rapid. But her passengers were scattered across the river. Brian ran the rapid and began hauling them out. Reaching shore, he walked over to see how White was doing. "She was standing in her motor well," he said, "and there was not a D-ring, there was not a bag, there was no gas can, there was nothing on her boat. There was only Georgie, and she was just standing there in shock. And I said, 'Georgie, what happened?'"

"I told them to hang on," she said. "They don't make passengers like they used to."

GOLD RUSH

Two packers working for the Powell survey in 1871 panned some gold dust from the river sandbars at the mouth of Kanab Creek. They returned to the town of Kanab, Utah Territory, in time for the New Year's festivities, which may explain how the story got out of hand so quickly. Powell's men announced they had found gold in paying quantities, and the report of a gold strike soon hit the newspapers. The 1872 rush was on, and an estimated five hundred prospectors funneled into the Grand Canyon. They rushed back to the rim almost as fast, muttering threats against the guy who started the rumor. Within four months, the excitement had ended.

Grand Canyon prospectors, circa 1901

CLINE LIBRARY SCA

BIGGEST NUGGET

Pete Berry, with his partners Ralph and Niles Cameron, sent a seven-hundred-pound (320-kg) nugget of 70-percent-pure copper from the Last Chance Mine on Horseshoe Mesa to the Chicago World's Fair in 1893. The mine continued to operate until 1907 when the copper market collapsed, making it too expensive to haul the ore out of the gorge.

Ore extracted from Last Chance Mine (not by these guys) was exceedingly high in copper content.

GCNP MUSEUM COLLECTION

51

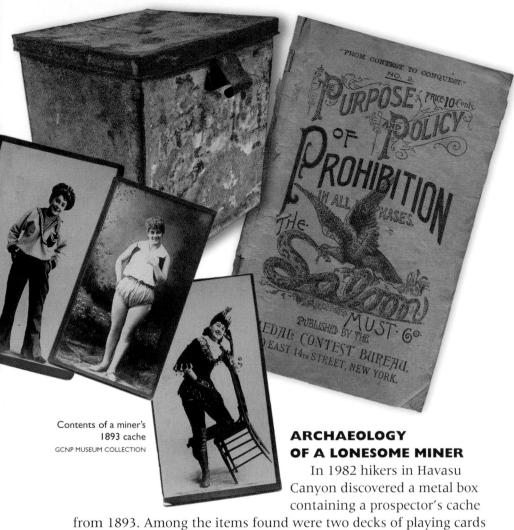

Contents of a miner's
1893 cache

GCNP MUSEUM COLLECTION

ARCHAEOLOGY
OF A LONESOME MINER

In 1982 hikers in Havasu
Canyon discovered a metal box
containing a prospector's cache
from 1893. Among the items found were two decks of playing cards
and various photos of women. The images, considered risqué in
those days, included a shot of two chorus girls, dressed in cowboy
hats and short shorts, striking provocative poses. Another indication
that human nature hasn't changed was a prohibition tract, titled
"The Saloon Must Go," wrapped around an empty beer bottle.

MOST DUBIOUS PLACE NAME

Woolsey Butte was named to honor King S. Woolsey, a pioneer
best known for having poisoned Yavapai Indians in 1864 with
strychnine-laced food. His fame also rested on having led an expedition that killed twenty Indians under a pretense of friendship
and then collected their scalps. Despite his reputation as an Indian
fighter, or perhaps because of it, Woolsey went on to serve in the
territorial legislature.

SACRED LANDS

The tradition of naming Grand Canyon landmarks after gods and goddesses began with geologist Clarence Dutton, an agnostic dropout from theology school.

CLOSE ENOUGH

Oddly enough, El Tovar Hotel was named after a man who never saw the canyon: Pedro de Tovar. In 1540 he was sent by Francisco Vásquez de Coronado to investigate the Hopi country but never went beyond their villages. Another officer, García López de Cárdenas, led the party that did reach the canyon. The name "Cardenas" was the first choice for the lodge, but it had already been taken by another Fred Harvey hotel.

GCNP MUSEUM COLLECTION

A RIVER RUNS THROUGH IT

The state of Colorado was named for the Colorado River. Unfortunately, at the time of statehood, the Colorado River did not flow within the state's boundaries. But a major tributary, the Grand River, did. To correct this oversight, the state officially changed the name of the Grand River to Colorado in 1921.

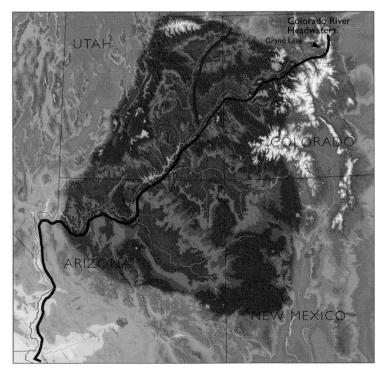

Colorado River Headwaters
Grand Lake
UTAH
COLORADO
ARIZONA
NEW MEXICO

COLORADO RIVER

GRAND RIVER, RENAMED COLORADO RIVER IN 1921

GREEN RIVER

U.S. GEOLOGICAL SURVEY

BETWEEN A ROCK AND A HARD PLACE

A sixty-one-mile (98-km) dirt road takes visitors to the spectacular Toroweap Overlook. The road narrows where it passes between huge sandstone boulders near the rim. The driver of a Greyhound bus, carrying students to view the gorge, was surprised to discover his motor coach was slightly wider than the space between the rocks. Wedged as tight as a cork in a bottle, the bus was extracted with difficulty.

MOST UNUSUAL CRIME

Three men were found guilty in 1995 of conspiring to collect butterflies illegally in the Grand Canyon and on other public lands. Agents from the U.S. Fish and Wildlife Service ran an elaborate sting operation to catch the lead poacher, who had eighty-seven Kaibab swallowtails in his possession when he was caught. The butterflies were thought to have been collected illegally inside Grand Canyon National Park. Hundreds of other rare and endangered butterflies were confiscated in the raid. The butterfly poacher received a sentence of five months in jail and a fine of $3,000.

View from
Toroweap Overlook
GEORGE H. H. HUEY

Endemic Kaibab
swallowtail
ILLUSTRATION BY JUDITH HODGES

OUTLAW HANG GLIDERS

The canyon's vertical terrain has tempted hang gliders since the sport was just getting off the ground, so to speak. It's against the law, but that didn't stop a pair of hang-gliding enthusiasts from trying their luck in 1972. Their plan was to launch early in the morning, land at a hidden beach, and hide their gear. But the ranger at Phantom Ranch, Bob Cornelius, caught wind of their plans and was waiting for them when they landed, citation book in hand. A couple of months later I heard the story from Ranger Cornelius, who said he made the lawbreakers hike back to the rim in cuffs—led behind his mule by a rope.

SCALP HUNTER AS FIRST TOURIST

With a bounty on his head, John Glanton led a murderous gang of scalp hunters north from Mexico in 1849. They fought a pitched battle against Apaches along the Little Colorado River and continued across the desert. Glanton thought he could reach the main Colorado River and follow it downstream, but mountain men in his party advised against it, knowing the way was blocked by deep gorges. A well-educated scalp hunter, Judge Holden, encouraged Glanton to continue north. The judge knew they would be forced to retrace their steps, but wanted to see "the greatest natural wonder of the world, the unexplored Great Canyon of the Colorado." The scalp hunters reached Marble Canyon and descended a tributary before being forced to turn back to the rim. By then, the judge had satisfied his curiosity.

WORST PREDICTION

In 1857 Lieutenant Joseph C. Ives led a military expedition that entered the Grand Canyon at Diamond Creek. The region he passed through on his journey did not impress him. "Ours has been the first," he reported, "and will doubtless be the last, party of whites to visit this profitless locality. It seems intended by nature that the Colorado River, along the greater portion of its lonely and majestic way, shall be forever unvisited and undisturbed." The number of visitors to Grand Canyon National Park in 2006: 4.36 million.

Engraving from Ives's report · GCNP MUSEUM COLLECTION

THE CASE OF THE BOGUS BOULDERS

The U.S. Geological Survey carried two imitation boulders down the river by boat in 1992. Made from fiberglass and polyester resins, they were meant to camouflage a water sampling station in Havasu Canyon. The real rocks, millions of tons of them choking the gorge, were rejected because of their weight. The $6,000 fake rocks were easier to handle; so easy, in fact, the next good flood carried them away.

A ROOM WITHOUT A VIEW

Commissioned by the Fred Harvey Company, architect Charles Whittlesey incorporated an unusual concept into El Tovar Hotel's design. He purposely oriented the rooms so they lacked good views, hoping to encourage guests to get off their duffs and walk outside for the full effect. Only three rooms on the north end have a view of the canyon.

El Tovar Hotel at the canyon's South Rim   TOM BROWNOLD

MOST UNUSUAL PARTY

Guests in formal attire attended the Midnight Croquet Garden Party at Phantom Ranch at the bottom of the canyon. Upon their arrival, they were greeted with a margarita fountain and a Mexican food buffet. If you get invited to such an affair, consider wearing a bola tie. The western string tie has been the official state tie of Arizona since 1971.

The string tie is the official state tie of Arizona

XANTERRA S. RIM, L.L.C.

56

FRED HARVEY BUNCH.   CANYON.   1915.

THE BOTTOM LINE

Fred Harvey revolutionized the hospitality industry with the efficient service and good values offered to travelers at his rail-side restaurants and lodges. He ran tourist accommodations at the South Rim for many years, and as a successful businessman kept his eye on the bottom line. A rumor circulating after his death claimed his last words were "Cut the ham thinner, boys."

GHOST DANCING

A religious movement known as the Ghost Dance took hold among the Hualapai, Havasupai, and Southern Paiute peoples in the late 1880s and early 1890s. The ritual dance, held in Havasu and Kanab canyons, was intended to restore the old ways and bring the dead back to life. During a sweat lodge ceremony, I once joined in as a Paiute sang a Ghost Dance song, or to be more accurate, I only hummed along.

MOST TIME-HONORED TRADITION

You can't visit Hermits Rest without ringing the bell. People will tell you to take seven paces from the mission bell and toss a pebble over your shoulder

HERMITS REST

without looking back. If you hit the bell, you'll have seven years of good luck. No on says what will happen if you miss. Have I tried my luck? Yes, years ago when no one was looking.

MOST BIZARRE WILDFIRE

For nine days, a fire crew fought burning deposits of ancient dung inside Grand Canyon's Rampart Cave. Thick layers of desiccated ground sloth dung dating back forty thousand years were on fire, destroying an invaluable record of past environments. What went unreported was the smell. To fight the fire you had to strap on an air tank, then enter the superheated cave, which was choked with acrid smoke and reeked with a skin-penetrating stench. My wife tells me it took a month for it to work its way out of my pores.

MOST EXTREME FISHING SPOT

A fisherman backpacked in from the North Rim, rigged a rope, then rappelled partway down the Tapeats Creek Narrows. Tying off, he hung while fishing the sheer-walled pockets of the creek. By the way, the cost of an Arizona fishing license is $18; the cost of catching an endangered humpback chub is $100,000. Every sport has its hidden costs.

THE MILLION-POUND MAP

In 1978 *National Geographic* magazine issued 10 million copies of Bradford Washburn's topographic map of the heart of the canyon. Printing it required 1,100,000 pounds (499,000 kg) of paper and 34,000 pounds (15,400 kg) of ink.

THE HEART OF THE
GRAND CANYON
Grand Canyon National Park, Arizona
Produced by the Cartographic Division
National Geographic Society
GILBERT M. GROSVENOR, PRESIDENT AND CHAIRMAN
NATIONAL GEOGRAPHIC MAGAZINE
WILLIAM GRAVES, EDITOR
JOHN B. GARVER, JR., CHIEF CARTOGRAPHER
in collaboration with the
Museum of Science, Boston, Massachusetts
BRADFORD WASHBURN, HONORARY DIRECTOR

LIMITED REVISION 1990

B A B
P L A T E A U

THE DAY GRAND CANYON CLOSED

For the first time in its history, the park closed on November 16, 1995, due to a deadlock between Congress and President Bill Clinton over the federal budget. Visitors were turned back at the gates and the park remained shut down until a compromise was reached on November 20, 1995.

Visitors have been turned away on only one occasion in the park's history.   GCNP MUSEUM COLLECTION (ALL)

REALITY CHECK

A young artist working at the South Rim asked the famous landscape painter, Thomas Moran (1837–1926), to critique his work. With a cigar in his mouth and a long white beard, Moran leaned close to the painting, giving it a thorough examination. And then he turned and walked away.

"But Mr. Moran!" cried the young man. "What do you think of my picture?"

Without pausing, Moran said over his shoulder, "I think it's framed beautifully."

Artist Thomas Moran returned to the Grand Canyon on many occasions, this time circa 1909.   GCNP MUSEUM COLLECTION

Park rangers Barbara Hastings and Eddie McKee

PHANTOM *Romance*

People have gotten married on the rim, on the trail, and on the river, which has a well-earned reputation as a marriage maker—and breaker. Some male residents of the canyon country enjoy marriage so much, they don't limit themselves to just one. John D. Lee, of Lees Ferry fame, had nineteen wives, and this tradition is still thriving in some communities north of the Grand Canyon. On the other side of the fence are lifelong bachelors like trail guide Captain John Hance.

The Lee family home at Lees Ferry, Arizona
GCNP MUSEUM COLLECTION

MY POOR WIFE

Never one to let the truth ruin a good story, Captain John Hance liked to tell visitors about the tragic end of the wife he never had. Leading a party down the trail, he would wait for the right moment to bring her up. Each time he mentioned her there was a catch in his voice, and he quickly changed the subject. He knew this would only heighten the curiosity of the women in the party. Sooner or later, one of them was bound to ask what happened to her.

"Oh, my poor wife," he would answer, letting the tears well up. "No one ever had a better woman. We were going down the trail, and the horse my wife was riding fell, and she broke her leg." His voice trailed off with a sigh.

"What did you do, Mr. Hance?"

"Nothing else to do," he said, "but shoot her and leave her there, poor woman."

Hance never married.   GCNP MUSEUM COLLECTION

61

THE RIGHT PLACE

"Many people get engaged at Phantom Ranch," said ranger Pam Cox. "One guy carried around a ring for two months waiting for the right place. He found it at Phantom."

GOING THE DISTANCE

One of the classic canyon romances involved Barbara Hastings and Eddie McKee, a young park naturalist. Only one thing stood between them—the Grand Canyon itself. McKee worked on the South Rim, while Hastings was busy collecting mammals on the North Rim. He would hike across the gorge on his days off to see her, until she finally agreed to meet him halfway at Phantom Ranch. While sitting with their feet dangling in Bright Angel Creek, he proposed, and the canyon couple were married on New Year's Eve, 1929.

It was a rare occasion when they didn't see eye-to-eye. After a collecting trip to Rampart Cave, McKee placed several specimens of ancient ground sloth dung on top of the piano for safekeeping. "No," Barbara said, drawing the line. "They look exactly like what they are!"

Longtime friend Tad Nichols (left) joined Eddie and Barbara McKee on a camping trip to Tuweep in 1968. CLINE LIBRARY SCA

DIVORCE, NAVAJO STYLE

Traditionally, Navajos took a practical approach to the breakup of a marriage. Since the woman owned most of the property, dividing it was simple. If a man came home and found his saddle outside the hogan, he knew he was divorced.

LOVE ON THE ROCKS

Grand Canyon pioneer Pete Berry first came to Arizona in 1887 to avenge the death of his brother, a saloon keeper killed trying to break up a barroom brawl. But the citizens of Flagstaff beat him to it. A lynch mob forced its way into the jail and shot the suspects when they resisted being dragged out and hung. Berry got the saloon and married May Hill Berry, his brother's beautiful but restless widow.

Town life had no hold on Pete Berry, so he spent much of his

Above: Pete Berry (far left) poses in front of his Flagstaff bar. Right: Pete and Martha Berry, circa 1895
GCNP MUSEUM COLLECTION

time prospecting in the Grand Canyon and developing the Last Chance Mine. His wife grew lonely and took up with a bartender. Hearing the rumors, Berry returned to town with blood in his eye. He shot his wife's lover in both legs, but the case was dropped when he informed the grand jury it had been accidental. A divorce followed in 1894, but Berry's saga didn't end there.

A few years later he went on a binge and was surprised to wake up in bed with his housekeeper. Before he could slip away, Martha Thompson produced a marriage certificate with his signature on it. He had no memory of the previous evening's events, but resigned himself to his fate. And this time the match took; Pete stayed married for nearly thirty years.

THE BOOK OF LOVE

Mule riders sat in the shade of a piñon, taking a water break at Cedar Ridge. One of the women asked the head wrangler if he was married. "Yes," he told her, "for three years. My wife's well educated but has to work below her abilities up here. She's a fine woman but she lived a spoiled life before I found her, so I made her send her credit card back to her father. But each time I threaten to send *her* home, he sends us more money."

Satisfied with his answer, the woman turned to the other wrangler. "Tell us about your life," she said.

He sat there, head bent without speaking as he pushed a pebble through the dust. When the woman repeated her question, he took a deep breath. "What chapter do you want?"

Onward & Downward: CANYON GUIDES

My first job at Grand Canyon was washing dishes for $1.20 an hour, and I felt uneasy taking that much. They let me live rent-free at Phantom Ranch in a stone cabin designed by Mary Colter and gave me four days off for every ten days worked, which allowed me to wander anywhere I wanted to go. At Phantom I met my first guides, the mule wranglers who brought in a string of saddle-sore tourists each afternoon. These cowboys had an expressive way of telling a story.

One evening, the staff was seated at a long table hidden away from the paying guests. It was one of the rare occasions when the cook served us steak. Old Pete, who had cowboyed most of his life, sat next to a young wrangler known as Re-Pete, who was eying his thick piece of meat, savoring the thought of it before digging in.

"If I stuck this steak on my head," he said, "my tongue would slap my brains out trying to get at it."

Old Pete gave him a weary look. "I've et so much beef in my time," he said, "I'd just as soon turn my back on it."

A few months later, I began working as a river guide. Boatmen and cowboys are different breeds, but they both tell stories that leave you wondering, "Could that be true?" And often it is.

On a run through Crystal Rapid, boatman Dave Wilson found himself heading into a notorious, boat-swallowing hole. He crouched down in the back of the motor rig and held on. The last thing he remembered was being catapulted into the air. He landed somewhere up front where he noticed his feet were bare. He had been wearing a pair of tennis shoes, laced up, when he entered the rapid. Making his way to the rear, he found his shoes. "They were

65

right where I'd been standing," he said. "And both of them were still laced up!"

By the way, never try betting a boatman. River guide Dave Lowry is known for choosing his words carefully—so carefully a group of passengers took bets to see if they could get him to talk. One of them walked over and told Lowry, "We're betting we can get you to say more than three words before noon." The boatman looked at him for a moment and said, "You lose."

My own experience as a guide taught me the world out there is so strange and unpredictable, you don't need to make it up. Tell it straight, and you'll still leave them wondering. But not every guide takes this approach, and many look to the original canyon guide, Captain John Hance, for inspiration. The fact he was never a captain didn't bother people any more than his claim to having first headed west riding on the back of a buffalo. All that mattered was his knack for telling a story and his ability to think on his feet.

A stranger once struck up a conversation with Hance and asked about the deer hunting. The guide said it was so good that he had killed three deer that very morning.

"That's wonderful!" said the stranger. "Do you know who I am?"

"No, I don't."

"Why I'm the game warden, and looks to me like you've broke a few of the game laws."

"Do you know who I am?" asked Hance.

"No, I don't."

"Well, I'm the biggest liar in Arizona."

John Hance's animated storytelling style was caught on film by early travel writer Burton Holmes.

Only once was Hance caught without a comeback. A little girl asked him how the Grand Canyon was made, and the guide told her he had dug it himself. But when she asked where he put all the dirt, he was stumped. Years later on his deathbed, he was heard to whisper, "Where do you suppose I could have put that dirt?"

In the end, the old guide fell victim to a common occupational hazard: if you tell a tale long enough, you start believing it yourself.

THE LIARS CLUB

Early canyon guides, W. W. Bass and Captain John Hance competed against each other for clients. And both did their best to uphold the reputation of the profession. "There are only three liars in the world," Hance said, admitting he was one of them. "And Bass is the other two."

SNAKE COUNTRY

Wrangler Patty Dunnigan was leading a string of mule riders up the trail when she encountered a hiker in his mid-forties.

"Are you the leader?" he asked, surprised to find a woman at the head of the party.

"No sir," she answered with a straight face. "But this is snake country, so they put us women out front."

Patty Dunnigan on the job

NPS PHOTO BY MICHAEL QUINN

THE LAND OF PETRIFIED SNOW

If a mule wrangler on the Bright Angel Trail points out a section of Redwall Limestone and calls it "petrified snow," rein him in. Runoff and wind have scoured the rock surface, exposing the pale limestone beneath. And if the wrangler calls some bird a "Grand Canyon canary," don't bother pulling out the binoculars. Guides may not give you an answer, but they'll definitely give you a response.

TOM BROWNOLD

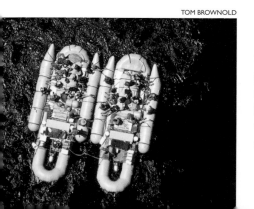

PARKING A BOAT

On Dave Wilson's first run through Crystal Rapid as a river guide, he got his motor rig stuck on a rock island in mid-rapid. Thinking quickly, he told his passengers, "Okay, hurry up and take your pictures. I can't hold it here forever."

RIVER PEASANTS

Early river explorers were reduced to eating musty flour and glad to have that. Passengers demand more these days. Take Princess Alexandra for example, who joined her wealthy friends on a chartered trip down the Colorado River. The Italian princess had no idea what she was getting herself into. "She had the impression," recalled boatman Eric Christensen, "we'd be making her bed with white linens."

Her plan was to hike down with her butlers and meet the boats at Phantom Ranch. The night before the trip, she presented the river guides with a simple demand. She wanted "a peasant" to carry her water bottle. A peasant? The boatmen politely informed her this was America, a country lacking in peasants.

Somehow she managed to descend the trail without a peasant, and, climbing into an oar-powered raft, she began her big adventure. The first difficulty occurred at Hermit Rapid when a crashing wave blew out a lens in her eyeglasses. She refused to continue riding with the same boatman, accusing him of having let the wave hit her on purpose. The princess got on Christensen's boat and unbuckled her life jacket to sun herself.

As they drifted toward Crystal Rapid he told her to buckle up. "I

Beyond QUESTION

There's no such thing as a dumb question, we're told, only dumb answers. On the other hand, there are exceptions to every rule. Take the following questions, actually fielded by guides and park rangers.

When do they turn the lights on in the canyon?

How many undiscovered ruins are there in the canyon?

Does the mule train have a caboose?

When are the services held at Shiva Temple?

Why did they build the canyon so close to the hotel?

Why is the Department of the Interior in charge of everything outside?

How old does a mule deer have to be before it turns into a mule?

What type of uniform does a cattle guard wear? Asked by a passenger on a tour bus after seeing a "Cattle Guard" sign.

forbid you to tell me that," she said, fully intending to go through the most dangerous rapid on the river with it unfastened. Christensen upped the ante. "You better get your boots," he told her. "You're walking out." After weighing her options, she reluctantly complied.

Later, as they floated down a quiet stretch, the princess told him she was bored and wanted a motorboat. When Christensen explained he couldn't do that, she demanded to be flown out. "Only in an emergency," he said. So the princess was stuck in the middle of one of the most stunning landscapes in the world. The river guide had noticed how oblivious the passengers had been to the beauty all around them. "They only discussed art and money," he said, "and art was only an excuse to talk about money."

Things came to a head when they made camp at The Ledges. The princess wanted her tent pitched where Eric had already set up the porta-potty. "She had her butlers move it near the tents of the lesser millionaires," he said. When he moved it back next to her tent, "she came up screeching."

"You are rude," she told him. And struggling to give more punch to the insult she added, "And you walk rudely!"

Passengers learn to do without certain amenities, but a river trip without a peasant can be especially hard on a princess.

"Where's the exit?" asked by a hiker who reached the ranger station at the bottom of the gorge. He had the mistaken impression there was an easier way out. The ranger pointed over the hiker's shoulder and answered, "The way you came."

How far below sea level is the river?

How deep is the river? Answers: "It comes halfway up a duck's rear end and over a fish's head," or

"Anything over three inches is deep enough to drown in."

A dark volcanic plug called Vulcans Anvil rises from the river a mile above Lava Falls. "That's Vulcans

Anvil?" a passenger asked the boatman. "Yep." The passenger looked puzzled. Glancing up and down the river he asked, "Where's the hammer?"

Vulcans Anvil   GARY LADD

Life-size bronze Brighty at the Grand
Canyon Lodge, North Rim

Brighty with visitors at Wylie Way Camp,
North Rim   GCNP MUSEUM COLLECTION (BOTH)

CREATURES
Wild AND TAME

When I find myself thinking about a place, it is usually in terms of the rocks, the rivers, and the lay of the land. But sometimes a landscape can reveal itself through certain animals. The people who live closest to a place, I've found, talk as much about the animals as the scenery. The Grand Canyon country is no different.

BRIGHTY THE BURRO

Many children first imagined a place called Grand Canyon by reading Marguerite Henry's *Brighty of the Grand Canyon*. Her book about a lovable, free-spirited burro became a bestseller and later a Disney film. It caught my interest when I learned the true story had largely gone untold.

The fictional animal was based on the adventures of a real burro, found alone at a deserted camp near the mouth of Bright Angel Creek about 1890. The loyal animal had waited in vain for more than a year for the return of two young prospectors who probably drowned trying to cross the river. Uncle Jim Owens heard about the burro and brought him back to his camp on the North Rim.

Brighty became a mascot to the locals, and regularly showed up at meal time for camp biscuits and pancakes. The burro loved children and let them pile onto his back for rides. He resisted being forced to work, but willingly helped a young boy, Bob McKee haul water for the tourists. Brighty even met Teddy Roosevelt and was given the honor of being the first to cross a new suspension bridge over the Colorado, completed in 1921.

Each winter over many years, the gentle animal descended into the canyon to his old haunts and then returned to spend summers on the North Rim. A touch of sadness seemed to mark the burro, who took no interest in other animals. He was often seen staring into the gorge as if waiting for someone to return. Surrounded by great beauty, the lone burro faced many dangers. Rockfalls and sudden storms were common hazards, and mountain lions were known to stalk him. But in the end, the human companionship he preferred turned out to be the greatest danger.

The gist of the story is this: In December 1921, an outlaw headed across Grand Canyon on foot, planning to lie low in the remote country to the north. Along the way, he caught Brighty, who was wintering as usual along Bright Angel Creek. The burro, now about thirty-seven years old, was made to carry a heavy pack to the snow-covered plateau above. As the two of them pushed on, breaking trail through deep drifts, a winter storm overtook them. They bivouacked the first night, and the next day the outlaw became lost in the blizzard. He hung his pistol and the pack containing all the food on a tree limb to lighten the load, but he was unable to find them later.

At nightfall, with their lives hanging in the balance, the outlaw spotted an empty cabin in DeMotte Park. The two of them took shelter inside, and the snow kept falling. Soon, another refugee from the storm, suffering severe frostbite, joined them. The snow eventually drifted to the rooftop, trapping the fugitive and the young storm victim for the winter. At this point the children's story parts from the fate of the real burro.

When the owners returned to their cabin in late spring, they found Brighty's remains. The outlaw and the other survivor had eaten the burro to keep from starving. But sometimes justice has a way of overtaking those on the run. Uncle Jim last saw the fugitive heading west across a vast roadless expanse, known locally as the Hurricane Desert. And then a late-season storm moved in, lasting for days. The outlaw was never seen again. Being alone and on foot in unfamiliar country, he likely died in the desert. The frostbite victim was taken to town and saved by the doctor.

Author Marguerite Henry with Jiggs, star of the 1967 movie
Brighty of the Grand Canyon   GCNP MUSEUM COLLECTION

Brighty lived on in the tales told by cowboys and trail guides, and a reminder of the solitary burro can be found at the North Rim. Inside the Grand Canyon Lodge, a life-size statue of Brighty sits on his haunches with his head turned to gaze out on the canyon. So many kids have rubbed his bronze nose for good luck, it's polished smooth. And sometimes, when no one is looking, I'll give it a rub myself.

KATHY THE TURKEY

A storm swept the North Rim in the early 1980s, blowing a wild turkey into Bright Angel Canyon. The lost hen found herself in alien surroundings without the security of the flock. Loneliness must have overcome her fear of humans. She began hanging out at Phantom Ranch and sometimes stirred things up by cruising through the campground or perching in a tree above someone's tent. Soon she became the mascot of the crew at Phantom, who named her Kathy.

TOM BROWNOLD (BOTH)

Often she stayed hidden in the trailside brush until a group of hikers passed by. Then she would pop out and tag along as if she were just another hiker. When they stopped and turned to look at the scenery, she did the same. For more than ten years, Kathy made the inner canyon her home, and during that time acquired a taste for long walks. Rangers heard reports of her wandering far up the trails on both sides of the canyon.

One day Kathy set out on her own again. She started across the Kaibab Suspension Bridge and ran into a string of pack mules and a wrangler crossing from the other direction. Undaunted, the turkey marched right through them, forcing the mules to dance left and right to get out of the way. When she finally reached the tunnel at the end of the bridge, something spooked her. As the turkey reversed course, the wrangler braced for more trouble. But Kathy simply jumped up on the railing and trotted past the skitterish mules.

Hiking into Phantom one summer, I talked with ranch manager Warren Tracy. Our conversation soon came around to Kathy. On his first Thanksgiving in the canyon, Tracy decided to lay on a fancy dinner for his crew. He closed down the dining room to outsiders and served a traditional meal with all the trimmings. Everyone took their seats, and as Tracy was about to carve the turkey, Kathy flew up and perched on the windowsill. "She kept staring in as we ate," he said, "trying to make us feel guilty."

CLEM THE ALLIGATOR

A rancher released a sixteen-inch (41-cm) alligator in a remote desert spring north of the Grand Canyon. When it was captured eighteen years later, it had grown to a length of eight feet three inches (250 cm)—having somehow survived on bullfrogs and unsus-

Clem measuring 8 feet 3 inches   BLM PHOTO

pecting birds. The Bureau of Land Management acquired Pakoon Springs, where the alligator lived, and the bureau wanted to avoid an incident where a tired and oblivious hiker stumbled onto a hungry gator. They brought in a team of reptile experts who finally caught Clem with a rabbit-baited snare in the summer of 2005. The desert gator now resides, if not fat at least sassy, in a wildlife sanctuary in Scottsdale, Arizona.

JAKE THE DOG

Some people come to the Grand Canyon to put distance between themselves and others. Mike Bacon, the last hermit of Hermit Canyon, was one such person. In 1972 he lived beneath an over-hanging ledge deep in the gorge. Whenever I passed through, I'd spend an evening talking with him and petting his big yellow dog, Jake. When fall came, he decided to take the dog and go to Mexico. He packed his few possessions and hiked out. It was night when they reached the South Rim.

After saying goodbye to friends, Bacon walked behind the Bright Angel Lodge for one last look at the canyon. His dog followed. At night the canyon absorbs all sound and light. Jake climbed on the low stone wall at the edge of the cliff and stared for a long time into the dark space below. Then he jumped. The next morning Bacon told me his dog was dead. "Jake," he said, "loved the canyon so much, he decided in his own way never to leave."

OLD POT

North Rim guide Uncle Jim Owens had a favorite white-and-tan dog called Pothound. He raised it from an orphan pup, feeding it warmed canned milk with an eyedropper. Whenever the guide moved camp, he wrapped the puppy in a piece of blanket and carried it inside a feed bag tied to the saddle horn. Uncle Jim often talked to Pot, who stared back at him, appearing to understand every word. Pot was the only dog allowed to sleep at the foot of the bed and later became the leader of the pack.

About the time Pot was old enough to drink from a dish, Uncle Jim took in an orphaned mountain lion kitten. The two of them lapped milk from the same dish with the lion kitten holding the pup down with its paw if he tried to take more than his share. When tired of playing, it picked up Pot by the scruff of his neck and carried him to the corner of the cabin where the two orphans curled up together.

Uncle Jim Owens and his favorite hound   GCNP MUSEUM COLLECTION

Uncle Jim guided Teddy Roosevelt on a North Rim hunt in 1913. To show his appreciation, the former president sent him a fine silk tent, lightweight and waterproof. When a forest ranger later came upon Uncle Jim during a heavy rainstorm, he found his five dogs huddle inside the silk tent and the guide taking shelter under a juniper tree. Uncle Jim loved animals and was one of those responsible for saving the buffalo from extinction. At the end of a long day he always fed his dogs first, his horses next, and himself last.

WALKING THE GOAT

A daily parade of hikers funnels down the Bright Angel Trail keeping park rangers on their toes. The rangers have encountered everything from mothers pushing babies in strollers to a tourist pulling his wheeled luggage behind him on his way to check in at Phantom Ranch.

Everything YOU KNOW IS WRONG

I keep a list handy to remind me not to take anything for granted. It's labeled, "Everything you know is wrong"—and it continues to grow. The list includes such things as this: The jackrabbit isn't a rabbit but a hare, the horny toad isn't a toad and doesn't have horns, the kissing bug doesn't have lips, the Redwall Limestone is gray, and there's no marble in Marble Canyon.

The naming of the natural world, I've come to realize, was a case of mistaken identity on a grand scale. Those who first entered the American West described the new lands they found with a vocabulary wrenched from the old. Sometimes they got it right; often they didn't.

Prairie dog

A few examples: the ringtail cat is not a cat, and the prairie dog isn't a dog—but it does bark. Some early travelers were closer to the mark when they called this rodent a barking squirrel. To hear the barking frog, which really exists, you'll have to go farther south in Arizona.

Strictly speaking, the North American elk is a wapiti. And adding to the difficulty, the term "elk" is used in other parts of the world to refer to a moose, and what we call an elk is known in Europe as a red deer.

The horny toad is actually a short-horned lizard, bristling with fleshy spines. And since it only mates once a year, you can disregard

Whenever the rangers think they've seen it all, another surprise turns up. A couple of miles below the rim, park volunteer Sueanne Kubicek spotted a man leading his goat down the trail on a dog leash. And a mule train was approaching. If the skittish mules spotted the goat, pandemonium was certain.

"What are you doing?" she asked.

"Well," answered the man from Kansas, "the sign at the top said, 'No Dogs.' It didn't say, 'No Goats.'"

Without arguing the point, Kubicek quickly turned him and his pet goat back toward the rim.

Short-horned lizard

the other explanation suggested by its name. This docile reptile can startle predators by squirting blood from its eyes, while the kissing bug will suck blood from a sleeping human.

The canyon tree frog lives in treeless canyons where its oversize toe pads allow it to cling to vertical rock. Those hearing its deep-throated croak for the first time often mistake it for the bleating of a mountain goat. The velvet ant resembles a fuzzy ant when scurrying along the ground, but this wasp has a painful sting and squeaks if handled. Yes, a squeaking wasp.

Sagebrush isn't sage, the seep-willow isn't a willow, and the creosote bush does not contain creosote, a wood preservative with a smoky odor. In fact, the creosote bush has a fine, intoxicating aroma that is released after a desert rain. While experts aren't certain how to classify the Douglas-fir, they agree it's not a true fir. Sometimes they simply call it "a taxonomic nightmare."

To avoid these confusions, scientists have come up with a precise, latinized

Canyon tree frog   TOM BROWNOLD

nomenclature, gaining accuracy while sacrificing the ability to carry on a normal conversation. The rest of us muddle on. Take junipers. Locals often refer to them as cedars, but no true cedars grow in the region. Come to think of it, most of the trees growing on Cedar Ridge in the Grand Canyon are piñon pine.

WAVERLY THE RAVEN

Forget Big Brother, it's the ravens who are watching your every move. No matter where you go in the canyon, they'll be somewhere nearby checking things out.

A few river ravens have become so notorious they've been given names, and a couple of those are printable. A raven even more brazen than most hung out at Stone Creek for many years. As soon as someone's back was turned, Waverly swooped in to steal anything edible or brightly colored. The raven earned its name from the crackers it loved to eat. It would stack one cracker on top of another until it had a pile barely able to fit in its wide-open beak. And then Waverly flew off with its loot.

Not only are ravens clever, they share the human capacity to deceive. Behavioral biologists have conducted experiments confirming ravens will not only fool other birds but will trick each other when it comes to food. While normally seen flying in twos and threes, ravens congregate at certain times of the year. In the winter of 1982–83, birders spotted a roost of eight hundred ravens below Grandview Point.

BEST BIRDING SPOT ON THE SOUTH RIM

Grand Canyon Village's sewage treatment lagoons are closed to the public, but birders flock to adjacent areas for birdwatching.

MONSTER BIRD

Condors in flight   ELENA MIRAS

Cave deposits high in the Redwall cliffs have yielded the bones of a giant bird known as Merriam's teratorn. It weighed nearly fifty pounds (23 kg) and once soared across the canyon on a wingspan of twelve feet (3.7 m). One of the largest flying birds known, it became extinct thousands of years ago at the end of the last ice age. Being a carrion-feeder, it did not survive the extinction of such mega-food sources as the mammoth and giant bison.

Before its reintroduction the California condor, with a wingspan of 9.5 feet (2.9 m), last visited the Grand Canyon in the late nineteenth-century. With only twenty-two birds remaining in the world in the mid-1980s, an effort was made to rescue this endangered species from extinction. Condors were successfully reintroduced to the Grand Canyon region in 1996, and visitors often see them at popular viewpoints. Having coevolved with herd animals, condors find themselves drawn to human herds.

ICE-AGE VAMPIRE

Scientists have excavated the remains of vampire bats from the canyon's Rampart Cave and adjacent sites. The bats fed on the blood of large mammals and left the region about thirteen thousand years ago, when their food source disappeared during the last ice age.

SNIFF TEST

Ancient packrat middens can date back more than thirty thousand years. Scientist Jim Mead has a handy rule of thumb for dating them. "If it has a super-acrid, sharp smell," he said, "then it's less than five thousand years old. If it's pungent but sweet, like a good wine, it's older than five thousand."

LAST OF THE JAGUARS

Prospectors reported that a jaguar mother and two cubs were taken in the Grand Canyon sometime during the late 1880s; another was killed by Havasupais on the plateau four miles (6.4 km) south of the South Rim in 1907; and a third, the last reported, was shot at Grand Canyon Village in 1932.

MONSTER MINNOW

The largest minnow in North America, the Colorado pikeminnow, once thrived in the waters of the Colorado River. Since it can grow to a length of six feet (180 cm) and weigh eighty pounds (36 kg), some pioneer anglers baited their hooks with small rabbits. Listed as an endangered species, its migration patterns have been disrupted by dams which also reduce the volume of flow, but populations of the pikeminnow in the upper river basin have stabilized. The fish was served as a main course for the Stanton expedition's Christmas dinner at Lees Ferry in 1889.

FLASH FLOOD DETECTOR

Biologist Larry Stevens has found a giant waterbug that scuttles out of a creek a few minutes before a flash flood hits. Able to sense the approaching flood, they return once the high flow passes. Trout appear to have a similar ability, leaving a creek when a flood is still a mile upstream and taking refuge in the main river.

Bark scorpion

STUNG, *Bit,* CHEWED

If you manage to avoid being pricked, poked, and needled by the desert vegetation, the next hurdle is the wildlife. It's a desert out there with migrating tarantulas, hairy scorpions and blood-sucking bugs, and chuckwallas inflating like balloons.
And then it gets serious.

Consider the tarantula hawk. This Pepsis wasp with a metallic blue-black body and orange wings, will hunt down a tarantula and sting it. Within seconds, the spider becomes paralyzed.

Then the wasp drags its helpless victim back to the spider's own burrow and lays a single egg on its abdomen. Several days later, the egg hatches, and the larva chows down on the still-living, but immobilized, spider. The sting of the tarantula hawk produces immediate, excruciating pain which lasts only about three minutes. Three very long minutes.

"If you get stung by one," said entomologist Justin Schmidt, "you might as well lie down and just scream."

MOST POISONOUS CRITTER

"The harvester ant has the most toxic venom of any organism in the New World," said biologist Larry Stevens. These red ants produce a poison more potent, ounce for ounce, than rattlesnake venom. But the miniscule amount they inject only causes a painful sting. And luckily for those sleeping under the stars, they return to the nest at night—about the time scorpions begin to stir.

A WITCH'S BREW

Only one scorpion in Grand Canyon is poisonous, but it happens to be a common one. The bark scorpion often tucks itself under the loose bark of cottonwood trees. But it can easily cling to the underside of the rock you just picked up or walk upside down across the ledge above your sleeping bag. Sensitive to light, it scuttles into dark corners as dawn approaches, and such a dark corner can be inside one of you boots. The venom of the bark scorpion contains a mix of at least thirty nerve toxins, often painful but rarely lethal.

At the end of a river trip, I pulled the boat into a beach at Scorpion Island in Lake Mead, a name that does not disappoint. That evening I joined a researcher hunting scorpions with a black light. When he turned it on, the terrace above camp lit up with the eerie green glow of several dozen scorpions within range of the dim light alone. On another night at the same camp, a thunderstorm moved in. Lightning bolts struck throughout the night, and so did the scorpions. Botanist Nancy Brian was hit half a dozen times, but luckily had only a mild reaction.

PINK RATTLER

Park naturalist Eddie McKee first identified the Grand Canyon rattlesnake on a hike down the old Tanner Trail in 1929. He spotted a rattler with an unusual pink color suggesting it might be an unnamed variety. Being a highly trained professional, he grabbed it with his bare hand and hiked out. And by the way, that is how most people get bit.

Back at his car, Eddie couldn't find a box or sack to put the snake in, so he held it out the window with his left hand and steered with the right. Unable to shift, he rattled up the dirt road in low gear until reaching the ranger station. The snake proved to be the first specimen collected of a type found only in the Grand Canyon.

Pink rattlesnake

TOM BROWNOLD

82

GRAND CANYON'S MOST DANGEROUS SNAKE

Rattlesnakes are born to bite, and they can strike without warning. About eight inches (20 cm) long, a baby rattler comes into the world fully fanged and loaded with venom. Since it hasn't learned to adjust the amount of poison to the size of the prey, it injects a full dose. The bite can be as deadly as an adult's bite, or worse. And not having developed rattles, a baby can strike without warning if surprised or threatened.

LARGEST LIZARD IN THE UNITED STATES

Found in the lower regions of Grand Canyon, the Gila monster is not only the largest lizard in the country but the only poisonous one. It grows up to two feet (60 cm) long and spends most of its time underground. Generally mild mannered, the Gila monster lives up to its name only if provoked, and then its jaws clamp down with the tenacity of a pit bull. The venom, a nerve toxin, oozes into the wound from grooved teeth, triggering instant and excruciating pain.

Gila monster

CRAZY WEATHER

When you live in a place where people wear sandals one day and snow boots the next, you learn to pay attention to the weather. A friend of mine, George Renner, always kept an eye peeled to the sky. He was a nomadic cedar-chest maker who set up his tipi outside of Flagstaff when passing through.

I stopped by his camp one day when dark clouds were leaning overhead. Renner was standing at his bench, using a hand plane to finish a board. He worked shirtless with a beard brushing his chest and braids hanging below his shoulders. Red suspenders held up a pair of Levi's so stiff with pitch he could stand them up in a corner, he bragged, and they wouldn't fall over.

"Do you think it's going to rain?" I asked.

Renner glanced over his shoulder and back at me, irritated by the question. "There's only two types of people who try to predict the weather in this country," he said. "Fools and newcomers." He paused a moment, looking straight at me. "I'm neither one."

Before heading into the Grand Canyon, I've learned to hedge my bets. I always check the weather report, but usually end up taking the same gear. If it calls for sunny days and clear nights, I pack for rain—just in case. And the "just in case" happens enough to make it worth the extra weight.

Out here the weather changes by the mile—and sometimes by the minute. Seventeen feet (5.2 m) of snow fell on the North Rim one winter while the South Rim, only ten miles (16 km) away and a thousand feet (305 m) lower, got half of that. At the bottom of the gorge, no snow was recorded. When it does snow low in the canyon, you don't expect it. A storm moved in one winter and caught our river party by surprise. I had to row through Crystal Rapid with the snow flying.

A year or two after visiting the cedar-chest maker, I pulled into the Marble Canyon Trading Post. A storm was building in the distance, and to make conversation, I asked an old Navajo working there if he thought it would rain. I should have known better. He squinted at the sky for a while before shrugging.

"I don't know," he said. "I didn't watch TV this morning."

THE CREEK THAT RUNS ONLY AT NIGHT

In the intense heat of summer, Pipe Creek disappears during the day only to flow again at night.

Pipe Creek   NPS PHOTO BY MICHAEL QUINN

HOT AIR

The hottest temperature recorded at the Grand Canyon is usually at Phantom Ranch. The bottom of the canyon is 20°F to 30°F (11–17°C) warmer than the rim. Air temperature increases about 5.5°F (3°C) with every one thousand feet (300 m) in elevation lost.

REDLINE

The temperature at which your brain will cook from extreme heat is 105°F (41°C). When core body temperature reaches that level, death is imminent.

DON'T SWEAT IT

Before embarking on a river trip, boatman Dave Edwards briefed his passengers at Lees Ferry. He emphasized the need to drink plenty of water, since they would sweat heavily in the desert conditions encountered. A passenger from Edwards' home state of North Carolina spoke up.

"Excuse me, David," she said, sweetly, "but where I come from horses sweat, men perspire, and women glow."

"Well," said the river guide, "down here you're going to glow like a pig."

IF A TOURIST COULD FLY

As a group of tourists prepared to ride into the canyon, Captain John Hance warned them about the incredible heat they would encounter at the river. "You cannot imagine how hot it is," he said. "Why, I'll give you my word, I have been down there when it was so hot it melted the wings off the flies."

"But," asked a lady from New England, "how do the tourists stand it?"

"Madame, I have never yet seen a tourist with wings!"

CASCADING SHEEP

During the heat of midsummer in 1906, J. D. Newman drove eight hundred sheep down from the high plateaus of Utah toward the river crossing at Lees Ferry. The animals had only a few miles to go before reaching the Colorado River, but they had gone three days without drinking and were desperate. Suddenly, the sheep caught the scent of water and stampeded. Driven mad by thirst, the herd veered off course and ran straight for a sheer-walled gorge hidden from view. The herders and dogs were powerless to stop them. The first sheep reached the rim of Cathedral Wash and tried to stop, but the momentum of those pressing from behind pushed them over the edge and the rest followed. Hundreds of sheep poured over the three-hundred-foot (90-m) cliff and fell to their deaths below.

LOVE SONG

Cicadas begin to sing as the temperature warms up. The electric buzz heard coming from the riverside thickets are the competing voices of male cicadas trying to attract a mate. Active during the hottest weather, they work up a sweat, literally. The desert cicada is the only insect known to sweat.

COLDEST TEMPERATURE RECORDED

In 1985 a temperature of -23°F (-30°C) was recorded on the North Rim.

MOST SNOWFALL

A record twenty-three feet (7 m) of snow fell on the North Rim in 1978.

MULES ON SNOWSHOES

To make sure a sure-footed mule remains sure footed on icy trails, the blacksmith replaces the normal mule shoe with one embedded with tungsten-carbide chips for a better grip.

Union Pacific work party snowed in on the North Rim walked to Roaring Springs and were met by a string of saddle mules from the South Rim. This photograph show them topping out at the South Kaibab Trail on Feburary 22, 1937.   GCNP MUSEUM COLLECTION

Robert Brewster Stanton

SCHEMES & Grand DREAMS

Some people stand on the brink of the Grand Canyon and can't help but think big. Big dreams, big schemes. I once took a Walt Disney executive down the river, and he seemed to enjoy every minute of the trip. But his enthusiasm wasn't for the scenery alone. Sitting in camp on the last night, he talked about what an incredible experience it had been—yes, the great views and yes, the exciting rapids. "But," he added, "it could be even better!" He began suggesting various improvements, such as constructing a cog rail to take boats back to the top of a rapid so passengers could run it as many times as they wanted. Sweeping an arm outward he said, "What Disney could do with this!"

Another wide-eyed dreamer was engineer Robert Stanton, hired to survey a river-level railroad through the Grand Canyon in 1889. Company president Frank Brown arranged for boats to be built and supplies gathered, but he overlooked one detail—life jackets. The expedition went downhill, or at least downriver, from there. Within twenty-five (40 km) miles of Lees Ferry and before reaching the big rapids, three men drowned, including Brown, who was pulled under by a whirlpool. The survivors abandoned the river, nearly dying on the climb out when a flash flood triggered a rockfall that nearly buried them.

A few months later Stanton returned with new boats. Despite bringing life jackets this time, the string of bad luck continued. Their photographer fell off a cliff, suffering multiple broken bones and a fractured skull. After carrying the unconscious victim to the rim, the crew got caught in a snowstorm. The photographer survived, but the expedition continued to be plagued by wrecked boats and the desertion of the head boatman. Stanton managed to complete his survey without further loss of life, but the railroad project was scuttled. To his dying day, the engineer insisted it was not only possible but practical to build a railroad along the Colorado River through the Grand Canyon.

Like Stanton, prospectors thought big. They probed every canyon

Guano mine in western Grand Canyon   NPS PHOTO BT ED CHAMBERLIN

tributary and promising ledge for a century, living on dreams and a grubstake. The mining period began with a gold rush in 1872 that never panned out, and ended with a more unusual strike that almost did. In the 1950s, inside a cave in the western canyon miners hit the mother lode. But instead of gold, it was bat guano.

The cave was estimated to contain 100,000 tons (91,000 metric tons) of the stuff valued at $15 million, an attractive sum. It made a high-powered fertilizer, but the problem was getting it to the buyers. The miners had to dig the guano, load it into immense buckets, and haul it to the rim using two miles (3.2 km) of cable. After investing several million dollars to extract only one thousand tons (910 metric tons) of guano, the company got a surprise: no more bat guano. They had grossly overestimated the size of the deposit. The mining operation hit rock bottom and shut down in 1960.

On an official trip, I decided to explore the abandoned mine. First, I climbed into the cave and found myself wading knee-deep in fresh guano from an active bat colony. Then I squeezed through a tight crawlway to see what lay beyond. By the time I returned to the river, I was covered head to toe in a slick coat of guano. Curiosity has its price.

Not far from the guano mine, on Hualapai tribal land, a rim-side attraction called The Skywalk now thrills tourists from Las Vegas.

Visitors cross a glass walkway extending seventy feet (21 m) over the canyon edge for a view straight down between their feet. And next year it might be something else. But the biggest dreamers are those who take the long view. When Teddy Roosevelt made a presidential visit to the South Rim in 1903 he hit upon a radical idea. "Leave it as it is," he said. "You cannot improve on it; not a bit. The ages have been at work on it, and man can only mar it."

THE GREAT KAIBAB DEER DRIVE

Sometimes the sheer audacity of a bad idea grabs the imagination and won't let go. An attempt to drive thousands of deer across one of the most rugged landscapes in the world falls into that category.

For years predators on the North Rim had been killed off in a misguided effort to improve the deer herd for hunters. By the summer of 1924, the mule deer population on the Kaibab Plateau had exploded and deer were starving by the thousands. The once lush parklands had turned into dust bowls, and every branch within reach had been browsed. The plight of the Kaibab deer herd drew national attention, and demands for action grew intense.

None of the experts could come up with a workable solution, and the politicians were growing desperate. The governor of Arizona was ready to listen when George McCormick of Flagstaff proposed rounding up five thousand deer and driving them across the Grand Canyon. Cattlemen, sportsmen, and conservationists soon threw their support behind the idea. Everyone appeared to back it—everyone except those who knew anything about deer or the lay of the land.

McCormick planned on driving the deer down the precipitous Nankoweap

Herd reduction memo, 1924

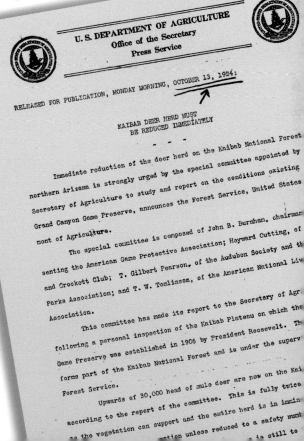

U. S. DEPARTMENT OF AGRICULTURE
Office of the Secretary
Press Service

RELEASED FOR PUBLICATION, MONDAY MORNING, OCTOBER 13, 1924:

KAIBAB DEER HERD MUST
BE REDUCED IMMEDIATELY

- - -

Immediate reduction of the deer herd on the Kaibab National Forest northern Arizona is strongly urged by the special committee appointed by Secretary of Agriculture to study and report on the conditions existing Grand Canyon Game Preserve, announces the Forest Service, United States ment of Agriculture.

The special committee is composed of John B. Burnham, chairman senting the American Game Protective Association; Hayward Cutting, of and Crockett Club; T. Gilbert Pearson, of the Audubon Society and th Parks Association; and T. W. Tomlinson, of the American National Liv Association.

This committee has made its report to the Secretary of Agr. following a personal inspection of the Kaibab Plateau on which the Game Preserve was established in 1906 by President Roosevelt. Th forms part of the Kaibab National Forest and is under the superv Forest Service.

Upwards of 30,000 head of mule deer are now on the Kai according to the report of the committee. This is fully twice as the vegetation can support and the entire herd is in immine ...tion unless reduced to a safety numb ...is still to

Trail and along the Horsethief Trail, a route he knew well from having previously escorted stolen horses along it. He would then swim the deer across the turbulent Colorado River and finally shoo them up the Tanner Trail to the South Rim. The plan was completely off the deep end. But the frontier spirit still lingered in those parts, and the idea of doing the impossible had its attractions.

The state of Arizona agreed to pay McCormick $2.50 a head for every deer brought across, and western novelist Zane Grey offered a large sum for the exclusive rights to the story. McCormick stood to gain thousands of dollars, but it all hinged on his ability to deliver the goods. In mid-December, the interested parties gathered near Saddle Canyon on the North Rim. Officials from various federal agencies joined park rangers to monitor the situation. The state game warden and his deputies were on hand to keep an eye on everyone else. And the event was not complete without the media. Legendary director D. W. Griffith arrived with six cameramen and a large supporting crew. They knew if they could get footage of the deer swimming the river it would be "a million-dollar film."

BILL HILLMAN COLLECTION

Zane Grey, attended by his personal valet and a Japanese cook, set up a comfortable camp. Being a novelist gave him one advantage—he had already written the story and only needed to flesh it out. For the actual drive, seventy-two Navajos and a couple dozen Paiutes were recruited along with thirty to forty cowboys and assorted greenhorns, all of whom were instructed to make noise as they herded the deer. Crews built miles of fencing to funnel the deer toward the canyon rim.

Thousands of deer roamed in scattered bands nearby, but the first attempt to consolidate them failed miserably. That evening, Gray Hat Charley showed up at the ranger cabin where the Navajo was asked if he had been able to round up any deer.

"Yes," he said, "drive deer, drive lots of deer."

When asked where, he swept his hand outward while making a humming sound. The deer had scattered in all directions.

The mood in camp had grown increasingly grim by December 16,

94

the morning of the final drive. Snow began to fall as the visibility lowered to fifty feet (15 m), and the temperature dropped below zero. The herders stretched across the valley in a ragged line, facing an uphill drive across broken, tree-covered slopes. And if somehow they managed to reach the rim, the real work of crossing the canyon would begin. Conditions improved somewhat by mid-afternoon, and the order was given to begin the drive.

Horsemen whooped and fired off blanks as the Navajos and Paiutes on foot jangled cowbells and yelled. They were pushing about two hundred deer ahead of them, but frightened by the noise and the converging lines, the animals panicked. Some turned tail and charged through the lines, forcing those on foot to scamper up trees or get run over. Other deer slipped around the wings, while a few bucks simply jumped the fence. Chaos reigned. "There's no way under God's sun," said game warden Jack Fuss, "you could herd 'em."

Frostbitten and discouraged, the beaters finally reached the head of the Nankoweap Trail empty-handed. Not a single deer had been rounded up. Cutting their losses, the cameramen packed up their

gear, while Zane Grey and D. W. Griffith took off for town in a Cadillac. Those in charge placed the blame on the unexpected wildness of the deer, a puzzling excuse.

The newspaper headline read, "Kaibab Deer Refuse to Herd, Animals Become Wild and Stampede Riders' Lines." The Great Kaibab Deer Drive ended with the discovery that wild deer had acted, well, just like wild deer.

DOHENY'S SCIENTIFIC EXPEDITION

Samuel Hubbard's idea of leading an expedition to Havasu Canyon in 1924 sputtered from the start. He planned to search for a petrified giant and the image of a dinosaur carved on a cliff face, hoping to prove Darwin

Mooney Falls   GARY LADD

wrong. But the National Park Service, which then had jurisdiction over parts of Havasu Canyon, refused to grant him a permit until he added a real geologist, Charles Gilmore, to the team. The Smithsonian Institution scientist enjoyed the monthlong outing, but refused to sign off on the expedition's claims. Hubbard interpreted a rather free-form petroglyph as a dinosaur and wind-scoured pockets in the sandstone as elephant tracks. Gilmore wasn't buying it. The petrified giant was also a bust, and Hubbard's report of a fossilized shoe sole from the Triassic Period, found in Nevada, didn't help his credibility.

Edward L. Doheny, one of the wealthiest men in America, bankrolled the expedition. His interest in Havasu dated back to 1880. As a young man he joined a prospecting party into the canyon and was a witness to Dan Mooney's fatal fall. Years later, Doheny made one of the first oil strikes in the Los Angeles basin. He went on to develop oil fields from California to Mexico, where he controlled vast holdings protected by an army of six thousand gunmen. Later, in 1924 he was implicated in the Teapot Dome scandal but beat the charge. Authorities accused Doheny of bribing an old prospecting buddy of his, Albert Fall, who happened to be the secretary of the interior at the time. A jury found Doheny innocent of giving the bribe, while a different jury found Fall guilty of taking the bribe. Good luck or good lawyers?

Feral burros were successfully airlifted out of the canyon by helicopters.   GCNP MUSEUM COLLECTION

WILD BURRO ROUNDUP

Prospectors led burros into the canyon and often didn't lead them back out. Those left behind went wild, eventually overgrazing sections of the park. To eliminate the feral herds, rangers decided to fly in armed teams. Environmental groups, including the Sierra Club and National Audubon Society, backed the park service decision. But when the story broke into the national news, animal rights groups molbilized.

Angered by what they saw as a policy of "burro-cide" protesters carried signs reading "Save Our Asses." As a compromise, the park service agreed to give the Fund for Animals the chance to capture as many wild burros as possible and put them up for adoption. The

Merry PRANKSTERS

Jack Fuss was looking for adventure more than a job when he agreed to work for W. W. Bass in the winter of 1918–19. He got what he wanted. "Old Captain Bass" had a mining camp at the bottom of the Grand Canyon, reached by a cable from the south side of the Colorado River. Fuss worked in the asbestos mine and built trail until his boots wore out. Since Bass was heading out for supplies, he promised to return soon with food and a new pair of boots. Fuss had to stay behind and watch camp.

With nothing to eat but prickly pear cactus and agave for three days, Fuss grew hungry. And then desperate. He decided he had to get out on his own or not at all. After repairing his boots with baling wire, he grabbed a medicine bottle, which would serve as his only water container. Bass had taken the cage across the cable, leaving his helper stranded on the north side. But Fuss rigged a seat from a hunk of old rope and pulled himself across the cable for nearly three hundred feet (90 m). The river churned below. It was a "terrific wash of slashin' and boilin'," he recalled, "and potholes and sluice holes and timbers and everything goin' down. And roarin' all the time."

Reaching the far side, he began the long trek up the South Bass Trail. His boots fell apart; he ran out of water. At three in the morning with his feet torn and full of cactus spines, he reached Bass' cabin. He scooped out a dead chipmunk floating in the water bucket, then dunked his head in, opened his mouth, and took a big swallow.

At first light Bass returned to his cabin and found Fuss collapsed on the cot.

"Well," he said, "I kinda thought you'd be here."

Fuss gave his boss a hard look. "I beat ya'," he told him; "I made it."

Bass's inner canyon camp   GCNP MUSEUM COLLECTION

effort began in 1980, with cowboys doing the rounding up and helicopters airlifting the burros to the rim.

In the lower canyon, they took many of the burros out by boat. The crew headed downriver to Diamond Creek whenever they had a dozen burros loaded onto the floating corral. No tranquilizers were used. To run a rapid, Russell Sullivan faced the pontoon boat upstream against the current. "I would run the boat backward," he said, "and go very slowly and gently." Remarkably, the burros never panicked and handled the rapids better than some passengers.

Burros removed during the eight-month rounup: 583
Burros transported by boat: 100
Cost per animal rescued: more than $1,000
Burros killed: 10 while being airlifted, 1 by falling off a cliff,
0 by drowning

MOST IMPROBABLE BOAT

The Bubble Boat, a clear plastic sphere supported by metal frames, was built in 1961 to carry a single passenger. It ran on an alternative energy source—a human-powered treadmill. The pilot had

The Bubble Boat, invented by Wayne Wilson, consisted of a round plastic bubble propelled by fins.

PHOTO BY GREG DIMMITT AND DAVID THOMPSON COURTESY OF MARRIOTT LIBRARY, UNIVERSITY OF UTAH to run like a caged squirrel to propel the boat, and it was impossible to steer in strong currents. "It simply bounced along," said Don Neff, the seventeen-year-old who managed to take the boat down the San Juan and Colorado rivers to Lees Ferry. Ignoring good advice to call off the attempt, the boat designer Wayne Wilson insisted on continuing through the dangerous rapids below. Taking command of the Bubble Boat, he made it as far as the first riffle. The distance covered? One mile (1.6 km).

LEARNING THE LINGO

Big Jim, a headman of the Havasupais, was often seen at the South Rim, proudly wearing a frock coat and a medal given to him by King Albert of Belgium. One summer, recalled canyon resident Ethel Metzger, he became friends with a dude from New York City.

The former policeman had Big Jim teach him a greeting in Havasupai so, the dude figured, he could surprise his other Havasupai friends. After struggling to get the right pronunciation, he finally decided to try it out. But when he walked up to a Havasupai and said hello, the man started laughing.

"What's the matter?" he asked. "Didn't I say it right?"

His Havasupai friend gently broke the news. "What you said was, 'Whiteman plenty big fool.'"

Havasupai headman Big Jim   GCNP MUSEUM COLLECTION

MOST OVER-HYPED STUNT

Professional daredevil Robbie Knievel boasted in 1999 that he would jump the Grand Canyon with a motorcycle. Unable to get a National Park Service permit for what the media billed as "The Grand Canyon Death Jump," he secured permission from the Hualapai Tribe to perform the stunt on tribal lands. Knievel ended up leaping two hundred feet (60 m) across an unnamed ravine on the rim of the gorge and landing hard. An impressive jump, but not over the Grand Canyon.

Legends AND Mysteries

The prank was a time-honored form of entertainment in the West, and newspapers were not above spoofing their readers. Serious reporting might run side-by-side with a good yarn. Consider a front-page story from the Arizona Gazette *announcing a stupendous discovery.*

LOST CITY OF THE GRAND CANYON

G. E. Kinkaid, it reported on April, 5, 1909, had found an ancient citadel during a river expedition through Grand Canyon. Hidden high on a cliff wall, a cave entrance led the explorer into a maze of rooms and passageways carved by hand and capable of holding fifty thousand people. He came upon mummies, copper tools, and tablets engraved with hieroglyphics, which suggested an Egyptian origin—or possibly Tibetan Buddhist. The article was vague on this point. Smithsonian archaeologists, it mentioned, were continuing to investigate the site.

An observant reader would have recalled an article about Kinkaid from the March 12 edition of the same newspaper. That story claimed he was the first man after John Wesley Powell to run the entire length of the Colorado. And if that wasn't enough to raise eyebrows, it added that the most interesting aspect of the trip was his having passed through the sluiceways of the Laguna Dam at Yuma.

Riddled with inaccuracies and wild exaggerations, the tale of the Lost City still attracts a following of true believers. Books, magazine articles, and hundreds of Web sites recount the story. The Smithsonian Institution repeatedly fields questions on the subject, and enthusiasts have even attempted to locate Kinkaid's cave.

LOST TRIBE OF ALBINO CLIFF DWELLERS

The Lost City falls into the same category as a story reported by the *San Francisco Examiner* in May 1890. The newspaper claimed C. L. Mosher had discovered a tribe of cliff dwellers in a branch of Cataract Canyon four years earlier. While searching for a mine known only to the Havasupais, Mosher had gone exploring on his own. He followed a narrow passageway into a hidden canyon where he heard a "distressing and terrifying wail," which filled him with dread.

Suddenly, "three of the strangest and most grotesque forms of humanity the eyes of man ever rested upon" bounded up the cliff. Four and a half feet (140 cm) tall, their hair bristled like the quills of an angry porcupine. Except for bright-orange pupils, the eyes and skin were white. Dozens of them scaled the surrounding cliffs and began rolling rocks down on the intruder. As he made an attempt "to placate the enraged dwarfs, the din of their terrifying gibberish increased in volume. . . ." At last a Havasupai chief rescued Mosher and led him back to the village—and the reader back to the real world.

ANCIENT UFO CRASH SITE

These days the spoof story has found its niche. The tabloid, *Weekly World News*, ran a cover story in 1994 titled, "4,000-Year-Old UFO Found in Grand Canyon!" It claimed scientists had investigated wreckage below Comanche Point and uncovered evidence that aliens survived the crash. The proof: rock art depicting "strange humanoid creatures with bulbous heads." Some of the canyon rock art is even stranger than the tabloid writers could imagine, but the chances of a wrecked UFO? I'll let you calculate those odds.

John D. Lee with two of his nineteen wives

LOST GOLD OF JOHN D. LEE

If John D. Lee had a gold mine, or a cache of gold nuggets as some believed, he took the secret with him to the grave. Even before a firing squad executed Lee in 1877, those closest to him were already hunting for his gold.

Lee had been arrested for his role in the Mountain Meadows Massacre, in which immigrants on a wagon train were slaughtered, and his first trial ended in a hung jury. Wells Spicer, who headed his defense team, was convinced there was something to the rumors of a secret mine. While Lee remained in jail awaiting his second trial, the lawyer set out in search of the gold.

Judge Spicer reached Lees Ferry and turned his powers of persuasion on

Lee's wife Emma, one of nineteen Mrs. Lees. When she wrote her husband to inform him of Spicer's search for his "hidden treasures," Lee advised her to have nothing to do with him. Instead, Emma agreed to outfit the lawyer for a cut of everything he might find—which in the end came to 25 percent of nothing.

The lawyer wasn't the only one looking for gold. Another indicted leader of the massacre, Isaac Haight, came out of hiding to conduct his own search. He also turned up empty-handed, but made another attempt in 1890 using the alias of "Brown." His guide was W. W. Bass who claimed he had been given a map by Emma. The canyon guide had tried unsuccessfully to find the lost mine a few years before, only to fall victim to a band of horse thieves. On this new attempt, they found the trail impassable, forcing Haight's party to turn back. During the maneuver, five burros plunged over a cliff to their deaths.

Many of the early canyon crowd got snared by the tales of lost gold. Pete Berry and Ralph Cameron, a newspaper reported, had left town to search for a lost mine. And Frank French, who married the widow Emma, teamed up with Seth Tanner to look for the mine. They thought an abandoned tunnel in Palisades Creek was Lee's mine, but they only ended up with a little copper for their troubles. Even George McCormick searched for the lost mine when he wasn't driving stolen horses across the canyon. For all their efforts, John D. Lee's gold remained a flash in the pan. No solid evidence of it has turned up. And being within a national park, those vulnerable to the lure of lost mines must search elsewhere.

A TUNNEL BENEATH THE RIVER

Navajos living near Marble Canyon have a traditional tale of a cave leading from one side of the gorge to the other, passing under the Colorado River. It was discovered when they were chasing a group of Paiutes who had taken refuge in a cave near the rim. The pursuers staked out the entrance, planning to wait them out. But the fugitives were later spotted making their getaway on the far side of the canyon, leading them to believe a passageway ran beneath the river.

Spelunkers have explored Paiute Cave and found no evidence of an escape route, but they did find the remains of old juniper-bark torches. Canyon expert Harvey Butchart believed the Navajo pursuers mistook a different group across the canyon for those they were chasing. When they let their guard down, the trapped party slipped away.

RIDING A COUGAR

Uncle Jim Owens, North Rim guide and government hunter, is said to have fallen from a cliff and landed on the back of a mountain lion. When the lion took off, he ended up riding it for several feet. Uncle Jim's reputation for bravery was unmatched, so the story could well be true. The only part that doesn't sound right is his falling off the cliff.

RIVER MYSTERY

In August 1869 the most daring exploration of its time ran into trouble. John Wesley Powell and his crew, battered by three hard months on the Colorado and Green rivers, faced what appeared to be an unrunable rapid. After a restless night camped above the pounding waters, three of the men chose to leave the river and take their chances on foot. William Dunn, together with O. G. Howland and his brother Seneca, headed up a promising side canyon now known as Separation Canyon.

"Through the Rapids" engraving from Powell's 1873 report

"Boys left us," reads Powell's terse journal entry. His three companions were never seen again. The remainder of the crew ran the rapid successfully and emerged the next day from the confines of the canyon. Powell had completed a remarkable first descent of the Colorado River, an achievement clouded by the breakup of his party. When Powell investigated the next year, he learned Paiutes had killed them, but that remains uncertain. No human remains and no rifles, scientific instruments, or expedition notebooks were ever recovered. An alternative version, hinted at in an old letter, has Powell's boatmen mistaken for federal agents by local settlers and executed.

THE THRILLING ADVENTURE OF CAPTAIN JOHN MOSS

A story from the April 9, 1877, issue of the *San Francisco Call* described John Moss as the first man to float through the Grand Canyon. A successful prospector and southwestern guide, Moss claimed to have taken a raft downriver from Lees Ferry in 1861, eight years before John Wesley Powell made his epic descent. Moss floated night and day without a place to land, passing through a gorge so deep sunlight only reached the river at midday. If readers were inclined to cut the frontiersman

John Moss with Paiute Chief Tercherrum near Fort Mohave, California, circa 1863   RUDOLPH D'HEUREUSE, BANCROFT LIBRARY

a little slack on this point, one fact should have stopped them cold. Moss ended his trip at Fort Mohave, he said, roughly four hundred river miles (645 km) from where he put in. And the time he claimed it took him? Three and a half days.

The editors of the *Arizona Miner*, a Prescott paper, weren't taken in when they reprinted the article. They let their readers know that Moss, who was well known in those parts, had been putting one over on the California newspaper.

NOBODY WILL FIND MY BONES

One of the greatest literary disappearances may not have happened in Mexico but somewhere in the Grand Canyon. Ambrose Bierce, an acerbic writer with a dark sense of humor, disappeared in 1913 when he was seventy-one years old. The most famous journalist of his day, Bierce crossed the Mexican border in a time of revolutionary upheaval and was never seen again. Most accounts of his disappearance say he joined Pancho Villa's army and died at the Battle of Ojinaga. Others think Villa had the Old Gringo stood up against a wall and shot. But solid evidence of his death is lacking.

Walter Neale, Bierce's closest friend at the time and first biographer, claimed he used the Mexico story as a cover to conceal his true destination. Neale, and recent biographer Roy Morris, present the intriguing possibility that Bierce actually disappeared in the Grand

Canyon. Long an advocate of suicide, the journalist discussed with friends his plans to kill himself before he became too infirm. He wanted to end it "the soldier's way" by shooting himself. Obsessed with death, Bierce had a human skull sitting on his desk and regularly attended hangings. He also found the topic of disappearances fascinating, and wrote a collection of stories called, "Mysterious Disappearances."

In 1912, the year before his own disappearance, he explored the Grand Canyon. He returned full of enthusiasm for the place and showed Neale a photograph of where he intended to die. The site overlooked the river where he claimed the vultures could not reach him. "Nobody will find my bones," Bierce wrote. Nearly a century has passed, and no trace of his remains has turned up.

LIBRARY OF CONGRESS PRINTS AND PHOTOGRAPHS DIVISION

MYSTERY SKELETON

In 1934 a river party pulled into South Canyon and proceeded to dig up a human skeleton. They played by different rules back then. The remains of the man they uncovered had dark hair and wore buckskin, making it difficult to tell whether he was a trapper or an Indian. One curious fact: both legs were broken, indicating he had likely died from injuries suffered in a fall.

Honeymooners Glen and Bessie Hyde
KOLB COLLECTION, CLINE LIBRARY SCA

WHEREABOUTS UNKNOWN

Glen and Bessie Hyde headed downriver in a homemade boat, attempting to set a speed record through the canyon. It was 1928, and people were pushing the limits. Glen had purposely not taken life jackets to heighten the thrill factor. Weeks later their boat was found snagged in mid-river, deep within the lower gorge. All gear appeared to be intact, and Bessie's diary was still onboard. A camera

The Hydes in their scow   KOLB COLLECTION, CLINE LIBRARY SCA

contained a roll of film with images showing Glen, Bessie, and the empty boat. The searchers surmised that Bessie had been holding the bowline when the current pulled her in above a rapid, and Glen dove in to save her. No sign of the missing couple has ever turned up, and the mystery has taken on a life of its own. Articles and books on the fatal trip have proliferated.

THE LAST LAUGH

When canyon photographer Emery Kolb died in 1976, he left behind a mystery. A skeleton turned up in an old canvas boat stored in the rafters of his studio garage, and the skull was found inside a Chase & Sanborn coffee can. After a delay of several years, the National Park Service handed over the remains to a deputy sheriff. A bullet hole in the right temple and a .32 caliber slug in the skull caught his attention. Clothes found with it dated from the 1920s, and a forensic anthropologist determined the bones were of a young man. The deputy now had an unsolved homicide on his hands—and the television program *Unsolved Mysteries* had another story.

Based on some preliminary thoughts by investigators, the TV people aired a segment linking the skeleton to Glen Hyde. But the sheriff's investigation finally concluded Kolb had found the skeleton years before in a shallow mine tunnel below the rim. And it turned out the photographer knew exactly what he was doing by hiding the remains in a boat. Kolb had always enjoyed a practical joke. He told a friend the skeleton would cause quite a commotion when it turned up after his death.

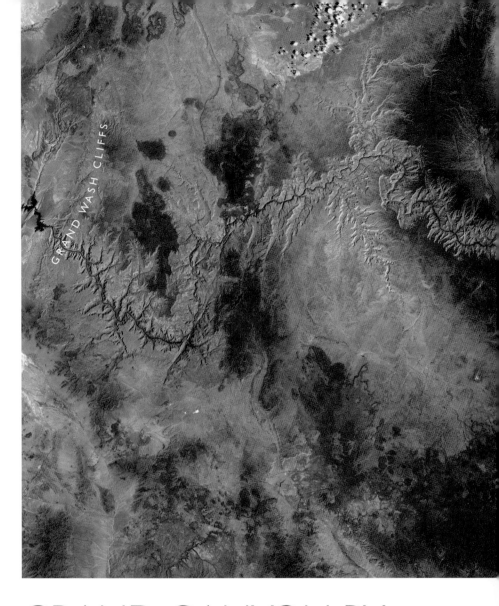

GRAND WASH CLIFFS

GRAND CANYON BY
the Numbers

*One way of coming to terms with a place where extremes are the
norm is to quantify it. Americans take comfort in numbers, a fact
recognized by the Inuits I lived with in the Arctic. Having a knack
for nicknames, they called Americans the "How-Many People,"
because we are always asking how many and how much. But*

LEES FERRY

FLAGSTAFF

U.S. GEOLOGICAL SURVEY

when geologist Clarence Dutton wrestled with describing the Grand Canyon in 1882, he realized numbers could only take us so far. "Dimensions mean nothing to the senses," he wrote, "and all that we are conscious of in this respect is a troubled sense of immensity."

CANYON LENGTH, THE LONG WAY AND THE LONGER WAY

Most sources give the length of the Grand Canyon as 277 river miles (446 km). That's the distance you would travel by putting a raft on the river at Lees Ferry and floating to the Grand Wash Cliffs at the canyon's end. If you walked the rim of the canyon between

109

the same points you would cover five times the distance. The length of the South Rim measures an impressive 1,373 miles (2,210 km), and the North Rim comes in slightly longer at 1,384 miles (2,227 km). Or as a mule wrangler put it in 1905, "God made it so damn big that you can't lie about it."

HIGHEST VIEWPOINT

The North Rim flares up to an elevation of 8,803 feet (2,683 m) at Point Imperial, overlooking the Nankoweap basin and Mount Hayden.

DAVID MUENCH

DEEPEST POINT

The vertical relief between the Nankoweap Rapid on the Colorado River and the North Rim at Point Imperial is more than six thousand feet (1,830 m).

At Mather Point, the gorge is nearly one mile (1.6 km) deep and ten miles (16 km) across. Or to look at it another way, it's eighteen Golden Gate Bridges wide and eight Washington Monuments deep.

HIGHEST WATERFALL

The seasonal flow of Cheyava Falls gushes from a cave high in the Redwall Limestone above Clear Creek and falls for eight hundred feet (245 m). When calculating official height, record keepers include cascading ledges and steep creekbeds below the falls, giving Cheyava

Cheyava Falls   LARRY ULRICH

impressive numbers. In dry seasons, the stream slows to a trickle.

Spectacular waterfalls suddenly appear during rainstorms on many of the canyon cliffs. Some of these flash falls are so high they turn to mist before reaching the ground. The highest waterfall with a permanent flow and a sheer drop is 196-foot (60-m) Mooney Falls in Havasu Canyon. Another unusual waterfall lies in Clear Creek where a stream-carved ledge deflects a plunging waterfall laterally. Canyon explorer George Steck called it, "The Horizontal Waterfall."

Folsom (left) and Clovis fragments

GCNP MUSEUM COLLECTION.

OLDEST ARTIFACTS

Birdwatcher Chuck LaRue found a fragment of a Clovis projectile point, about twelve thousand years old, on the South Rim. A partial Folsom point, dating back ten thousand years, turned up in Marble Canyon. No other evidence of these

early hunters has been recorded in the national park. Folsom people hunted giant ice age bison and the Clovis people had a taste for mammoth. What they were doing in the canyon is anybody's guess.

Prehistoric bridge GARY LADD

OLDEST BRIDGE

Wood taken from an ancestral Puebloan footbridge on a cliff above President Harding Rapid has been dated to AD 900. But since these prehistoric people likely used salvaged driftwood, the bridge could easily be younger. Only three bridges span the Colorado River in the Grand Canyon. A highway bridge crosses Marble Canyon 4.5 miles (7.2 km) below Lees Ferry, and two footbridges cross at Bright Angel Creek near river mile 88.

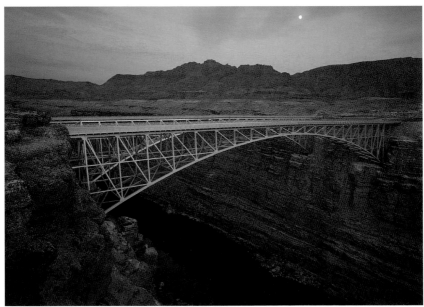

Navajo Bridge crosses the Colorado River near Lees Ferry GARY LADD

LONGEST TRAIL

The Tonto Trail begins at Red Canyon in the east, follows a broad bench known as the Tonto Platform, and ends about ninety-five miles (153 km) later at Garnet Canyon.

MOST MILES HIKED BELOW THE RIM

Superhiker Harvey Butchart made his first canyon hike when he was a thirty-eight-year-old math professor and his last at the age of eighty-two. In between, he logged some twelve thousand miles (19,000 km) while pioneering new backcountry routes and solving historical mysteries. Hikers Jim Ohlman and Ken Walters, protégés of Dr. Butchart, have matched his record.

MOST MILES RIDDEN MULEBACK

For years, packer Ross Knox made daily trips from the South Rim to Phantom Ranch, while leading a pack string and writing poetry. He ended up riding 40,000 miles (64,000 km), but some pieces of tack have seen even more miles. The caption on a dude saddle displayed at Kolb Studio notes it was sat in for at least 54,600 miles (87,800 km) over a span of twenty years.

Ross Knox   NPS PHOTO BY MICHAEL QUINN

Lava flows near Toroweap in western Grand Canyon   GARY LADD

SHORTEST RIM-TO-RIVER TRAIL

This hot, steep, and sometimes confusing route of Lava Falls Trail descends 1.5 miles (2.4 km) from Toroweap Valley to the river. Going from river to rim, the trail feels twice as long.

FASTEST RIM-TO-RIM RUN

Allyn Cureton set a record in 1981, running down the South Kaibab Trail and up the North Kaibab in three hours and seven minutes.

That's nearly twenty-one trail miles (34 km). Note: Racing from rim to rim is not recommended. Not only do you miss the scenery around you, it can be deadly.

FASTEST RIM-TO-RIM AND BACK AGAIN

A month after setting the rim-to-rim record, Allyn Cureton accidentally set the double rim-to-rim record while training for another run. He used the South and North Kaibab trails, covering more than forty-two miles (78 km) in seven hours and fifty-one minutes. See note in previous entry.

SLOWEST RIM-TO-RIVER TRIP

Charles Russell's attempt to run the Colorado River proved so stressful that he ended up sitting alone in camp muttering to himself. After losing a boat, he ordered another built and shipped to the South Rim. In 1915 he placed the sixteen-foot (5-m) steel boat on a dolly and with a crew of two began wheeling it down the Bright Angel Trail. Whenever they encountered a mule train, they covered the boat with canvas to keep the mules from spooking. They finally reached the river a week after leaving the rim.

LONGEST LAUNDRY TRIP

During dry spells, Ada Bass rode down the South Bass Trail to the river, did the laundry, and returned to the rim three days later.

A graduate of the Boston Conservatory of Music, Ada married canyon guide W. W. Bass and became a classic pioneer woman. She not only raised a family two days from the nearest town, she also ran the tourist camp, did the washing and cooking, and sometimes

Ada Bass at Bass Camp on the South Rim

guided guests into the canyon. But she never gave up her piano and insisted it go with her each time the family moved.

LONGEST GEOLOGICAL STEP

A single step on the Bright Angel Trail at the Great Unconformity spans 1.2 billion years of geologic time. Lying between the Tapeats Sandstone and Vishnu Schist, the unconformity represents the missing rock layers found in other regions but eroded away long before the Grand Canyon formed.

A hiker descending the South Kaibab Trail goes from 270-million-year-old rocks at the rim to 1.7-billion-year-old rocks at the river. The canyon walls record such an immense span of time, each step down the trail takes you back in geologic time more than 100,000 years.

LONGEST GRAND CANYON RIVER

From its headwaters in the Rocky Mountains, the Colorado River runs 1,450 miles (2,333 km) to the Gulf of California, with 277 miles (446 km) of it lying within Grand Canyon. The river loses

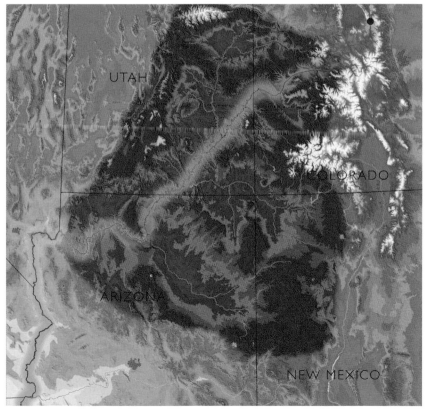

The Colorado River flows 1,450 miles from its headwaters in the Rocky Mountains of Colorado to the Gulf of California.   U.S. GEOLOGICAL SURVEY

2,100 feet (640 m) in elevation through the canyon on a gradient twenty-five times steeper than the Mississippi. Half of that loss occurs in 165 rapids. The river averages three hundred feet (90 m) wide but pinches down to seventy-six feet (23 m) at Granite Narrows.

SHORTEST GRAND CANYON RIVER

Among the world's shortest rivers, Thunder River gushes from a cave opening in a spectacular waterfall and flows for only half a mile (0.8 km)—twice that if you include the mapped underground passageways. And it may be the only river in the world to flow into a creek, Tapeats Creek.

Thunder River   LARRY ULRICH

GREATEST VERTICAL DROP IN A RAPID

From entry to exit, Hance Rapid drops thirty rock-choked feet (9 m).

MOST DANGEROUS RAPID

Six fatalities have occurred in Crystal Rapid, either by drowning or cardiac arrest. Like Lava, it's rated 10 on a scale of 10—and 10+ if you have a bad run.

LONGEST FIFTEEN SECONDS

Rated 10 on a scale of 10, Lava Falls Rapid drops fourteen feet (4 m) over

A wet ride through Lava Falls   LEON WERDINGER

a distance of one hundred yards (90 m). For those who have been washed out of a boat and dragged under the turbulent water, the fifteen-second run can feel like a lifetime.

LONGEST STAY BELOW THE RIM

National Park Service employee Bruce Aiken and his wife Mary once remained at their home below the North Rim near Roaring Springs for six months without leaving the canyon. "When we finally hiked out and got in a car," Mary said, "it was like a Disney ride— woo-ooo! And the big, wide-open spaces came at us all at once."

FASTEST OAR-POWERED RUN

High water flowed through Grand Canyon in the summer of 1983. River guides Kenton Grua, Rudi Petschek, and Steve Reynolds knew high water meant fast water and decided to take advantage of it and set a new speed record. The three boatmen launched a wooden dory at Lees Ferry on the biggest water they had ever experienced—72,000 cubic feet per second (2,040 m³/second), when normal flows run about 10,000 cfs

Kenton Grua in Marble Canyon   FRED HIRSCHMANN

(285 m³/sec.). Despite flipping end-over-end in Crystal Rapid, they rowed out the bottom of the gorge thirty-six hours and thirty-eight minutes later. A standard oar-powered trip takes two weeks.

OLDEST ROCK

Formed 1.84-billion years ago, the Elves Chasm Pluton is found in the Inner Gorge, which consists primarily of 1.75-billion-year-old Vishnu Schist. The carving of the Grand Canyon happened much more recently.

Elves Chasm

JACK DYKINGA

Geologists say the canyon as we know it, with the river flowing in its present course, is at least 5.6 million years old. Canyon cutting by the Colorado River has removed one thousand cubic miles (4,168 km³) of rock.

YOUNGEST ROCKS

Volcanic vents in the western canyon have been active during the last 638,000 years. Lava flowing from them has cascaded over the rim of the western canyon more than a dozen times, turning the river to steam and forming immense basalt dams.

Travertine continues to be formed in springs and creeks laden with calcium and magnesium carbonates, calcium sulfate, and magnesium chloride. The minerals are carried in solution until they meet the dry canyon air. Carbon dioxide evaporates causing the carbonates to separate from the water, coating the streambed with travertine.

The Kaibab Formation, occurring as the rimrock for most of the canyon, consists of limestones and shales deposited 270 million years ago. Formed three hundred feet (91 m) below sea level, the rock can now be found at elevations above eight thousand feet (2,440 m).

Numbers in *italics*
indicate illustration

Aiken, Bruce, 117; Mary
117
airplane, 25, 36
alligator, 74
Apache, 55
Apollo, 46
Arctic, 33, 108
astronaut, 46, *46*
Atlantic, 33
Ayer, Edward, 18;
Emma, 19; Point, 19

Bacon, Mike, 74
Baja California, 33
basalt, 119
Bass, Ada, 114, *114*;
Camp, 97; Trail 17,
32, 97, 114; W.W.,
7, 17, *17*, 36, *36*, 67,
97, 103, 114
bat, 79, 92
Beckman, Billy, 27
Beer, Bill, 23, *23*
Benson, Robert, 32
Berry, Martha, *63*; Pete,
51, 62, 63, *63*, 103
Bierce, Ambrose,
105–106, *106*
Big Jim, 99, *99*
Bishop, Frank, 21, *22*
bison, see buffalo
Black Canyon, 20
Blake, Robert, 30
blizzard, 30, 72
brawl, 62
Brian, Nancy, 82; Terry,
50, 98
bridge, 47, 71, 73,
110, 112, *112*; foot
bridge, 19, 112, *112*

Bright Angel, Canyon,
19, 42, 73; Creek,
42, 47, *47*, 62, 71,
72, 112; Lodge,
14, 74; Point, 11;
Spring, 41; Trail, 45,
67, 75, 114–115
Brighty, *70*, 71–72, *72*
Brooks, James, 40
Brown, Frank, 91
bubble boat, *97*, 97–98
buffalo, 39, 40–41, *41*,
66, 75
Buffalo Jones, 46
burro, 7, 19, 45, 46,
71–72, 96, *96*, 103
Butchart, Harvey, 103,
113
butterfly, 54, *54*

Cameron, Ralph, 51, 103
canoe, 33–35, *33*, *35*
Canyonlands National
Park, 32
Cape Royal Road, 31
Cárdenas, García López
de, 14–15, 53
Cataract, 24
Cataract Canyon, 32,
41, 101
Cathedral Wash, 87
cave, 28–30, *29*, 58, 62,
78–79, 92, *92*, 101,
103, 110, 116, *116*
Cedar Ridge, 63, 77
cemetery, Grand
Canyon, *25*, 118
Cheyava Falls, 28,
110–111, *111*
Chicago World's Fair, 51
Chilkoot Pass, 33
chorus girl, 52, *52*
Christensen, Eric, 68–69
chuckwalla, 81

cicada, 88, *88*
Civilian Conservation
Corps, 39, 47, *47*
Clear Creek, 28,
110–111
Clem, 74, *74*
Clinton, President, 59
Clover, Elzada, 24, *24*
Clovis projectile point,
111, 111–112
Cobb, Irvin S., 18
Coconino Sandstone,
28, *48*
Collingwood, George, 12
Colorado River, 9,
15–16, 19–22,
24–25, 33–34,
39–40, 53, 55, 79,
87, 91, 94, 97–98,
103–104, 110, 112,
112, 114–115, 119
Colter, Mary, 64
condor, 78–79, *78*
Congress, U.S., 22, 59
conquistadors, 114–115,
114
copper, 19, 51, 101, 103
Cornelius, Bob, 55
Coronado, Francisco
Vásquez de, 14, 53
cowboy, 24, 40, 52,
64–65, 72, 94, 96
Cox, Pam, 62
Crystal Rapid, 43, 49,
65, 67, 68, 86, 116,
117

Daggett, John, 23, *23*
Dale, Bruce, 11
Dam Site Trail, 40
darkroom, 44–45, *44*
deer, 66, 68, 76, 93–95
DeMotte Park, 72
Desert View, 15, 39

Diamond Creek, 18, 55
dinosaur, 95–96
Disney, 71, 91, 117
divorce, 37, 62, 63,
dog, 9, 21, 41, 46, 74,
    75, 75, 76, 87
Doheny, Edward, 27,
    95–96
dory, 10–11, 10, 117
dung, 58, 62
Dunn, William, 104
Dunnigan, Patty, 67, 67
Dutton, Clarence, 53,
    109

Eddy, Clyde, 24
Edwards, Dave, 87
Elaine's Castle, 32
elk, 76
El Tovar Hotel, 11, 53,
    56, 56
Elves Chasm, 117, 138
expedition, 14, 21, 21,
    22, 34–35, 52, 55,
    79, 91, 95–96, 101,
    104
explorer, 9, 14–15, 29,
    68, 101, 111
Explorer, the, 20, 20

Fall, Albert, 96
Falls Cave, 29–30
Farlee, Julius, 18
fatal, 17, 96, 107, 116
Federal Aviation
    Administration, 25
Ferrall, Louisa, 19
fire, 22, 37, 46, 50, 58,
    95
Flagstaff, 18, 24, 62, 63,
    84, 93
flood, 29, 39–40, 42–43,
    56, 79, 91

Folsom projectile point,
    111–112, 111
Fortney, Linda, 41
fossil, 48, 96
French, Frank, 103
frog, 74, 76–77, 77
Fuss, Jack, 13, 95, 97

Galloway, Nathaniel,
    23, 23
Gandy, Marvin, 37
Garcés, Francisco, 15, 15
Ghost Dance, 57
Gila monster, 83, 83
Gilmore, Charles, 48, 96
Glanton, John, 55
Glen Canyon, 21, 22, 32
Glover, K.J., 42
goat, 75, 76–78
gold, 14–15, 19, 39, 51,
    92, 102–103
Grand Canyon National
    Park, 39, 54, 55, 96
Grand Canyon Village,
    78, 79
Grand River, 53
Grand Wash Cliffs, 16,
    19–20, 109
Grandview Point, 19, 78
Granite Narrows, 116
Great Lakes, 33
Great Unconformity,
    115
Green River, 21, 21, 53,
    104
Grey, Zane, 94–95
Greyhound bus, 54
Griffith, D.W., 94–95
Grua, Kenton, 19, 117,
    117
guano, 92
Gulf of California, 115

Hamblin, Jacob, 16, 22
Hance, John, 9, 18, 18,
    19, 61, 61, 66–67, 66,
    87; Rapid 116
hang glide, 54
Harvey, Fred, 53, 56, 57
Harvey Meadow, 40
Hassemer, Jerry, 30
Havasu Canyon, 15, 27,
    52, 56, 57, 95–96,
    111
Havasupai, people, 15,
    27, 36, 41, 46, 47,
    47, 57, 79, 99,
    101–102;
    Reservation, 49, 49
helicopter, 42, 42, 48,
    49, 96–97, 96
Hellhole Bend, 39–40
Henderson, Roger, 37
Henry, Marguerite, 71,
    72
Hermit, Canyon, 74;
    Rapid, 68; Trail, 48
Hermits Rest, 57
hogan, 62
Hogan, Dan, 19, 27–28
Hogan's Slide, 28, 28
Holden, Judge, 55
Holmes, Burton, 66
Holy Grail Temple, 36
Hoover Dam, 20
Hopi, 14–15, 16, 20–21,
    53; mesas, 15; trail,
    39; village, 15, 16
Horn Creek Rapid, 11
Horseshoe Mesa, 51
Horsethief Trail, 94
hospital, 31–32, 37, 40
Howe, Jon, 29
Howland, O.G., 104
Hualapai, 57, 92, 99
Hubbard, Samuel,
    95–96

Hubbell Butte, 30
Hubbell, Lorenzo, 19, *19*
Hummingbird Trail, 27–28, *28*
humpback chub, 58
Humphreys, Alphonso, 27
Hurricane Desert, 72
Hyde, Bessie, 24, 106–107, *106*
Hyde, Glen, 106–107, *106*

ice age, 78, 79, 112
Indian Garden, 44–45, *44*
Inner Gorge, 117
Ives, Lt. Joseph C., 20, *20*, 55

Jackass Canyon, 20
jaguar, 79
Jotter, Lois, 24, *24*

Kaibab, deer drive, 93–95; Formation, 119; Limestone, 28; Plateau, 16, 93; suspension bridge, 47, 73; swallowtail, 54, *54*; Trail, 37, 46, 47, *88*, 113, 114, 115
Kanab, Canyon, 57; Creek, 51; Utah, 19
kissing bug, 76–77
Knievel, Robbie, 99
Knox, Ross, 113, *113*
Kolb, Blanche, *44*; Ellsworth, *25*, 28–29; Emery, 28–29, *29*, 45, 107; Studio, 113
Kruger, Verlen, 33–35, *33*, *35*

Kubicek, Sueanne, 76

Landick, Steve, 33–35, *33*, *35*
Last Chance Mine, 51, *51*, 63
Lava Creek, 30
Lava Falls Rapid, 11, 48–49, 69, 116, *116*; Trail, 113
Lee, Emma, 103; John D., 61, 102–103, *102*
Lees Ferry, 16, 19–20, 22, 35, 61, *61*, 79, 87, 91, 98, 102–103, 104, 109, 112, 117
Lippincott, Oliver, 24, *24*
Little Colorado River, 25, 39–40, 55, 116
lizard, Gila, 83, *83*; short-horned, 76–77, *77*
Lookout Point, 17
Lowry, Dave, 66

Mackenzie River, 33
mail, 37, 49, *49*
Marble Canyon, 29, 35, 55, 76, 103, 111, 112, *117*; Trading Post, 86
Mather Point, 110
McCormick, George, 93–94, 103
McKee, Barbara, *60*, 62, *62*; Bob 71; Eddie, *60*, 62, *62*, 82
Mead, Jim, 79
Mexico, 32, 55, 74, 96, 105
mine, 51, *92*, 97, 101–103, 107
miner, 27, 52, 92, 105
Mississippi River, 33, 116

Moab, Utah, 33
Mohave, Fort, 105
Moody Trail, 39
Mooney, Dan, 27, 96; Falls, *26*, 95, 111
Moran, Thomas, 22, 59, *59*
Mormon, 16, 18, 22
Morris, Roy, 105
Moss, John, 105, *105*
motor rig, 42, *43*, 49, 65, 67, 96
motorcycle, 99
Moulton, Horace, 39–40
mountain lion, 46, 71, 75, 104
Mountain Meadows Massacre, 102
Muav Saddle, 32, *32*
mule, 37, *37*, 45, 46, 49, *49*, 55, 63, 64, 67, 68, 73, 76, 88, *88*, 110, 113, 114
mummy, 101

Nankoweap basin, 110; Rapid, 110; Trail, 30, 93, 95
National Geographic, 11, 58
National Park Service, *42*, 43, 96, 99, 107, 117
Navajo, 16, 19, 22, 62, 86, 94–95, 103; bridge, *112*
Neale, Walter, 105–106
Neff, Don, 98
Nevills, Norm, 24
New Mexico, 32
Newman, J.D., 87
Nichols, Tad, *62*
North America, 33, 76, 79, 125

North Bass Trail, 32

North Rim, 19, 22, 25, 28, 30–31, 32, 40, 46, 58, 62, 71, 72, 74, 75, 86, 88, 93–95, 104, 110, 117

Northern Arizona University, 30

O'Neill, Buckey, 37; Butte, 37

Ohlman, Jim, 113

Orphan Mine, 19, 27

Ott, Bill, 20

Owens, James T. (Uncle Jim), 40–41, 40, 41, 46, 71, 74–75, 75, 104

Packard, Bob, 30–31

Paiute, 16, 19, 21, 57, 94–95, 103, 104, 105

Pakoon Springs, 74

Palisades Creek, 103

park ranger, 39, 43, 48, 60, 68, 75, 94

Pattie, James Ohio, 15

Peach Springs, 18

petroglyph, 96

Phantom Ranch, 37, 46, 47, 47, 49, 55, 56, 62, 64, 68, 73, 75, 87, 113, 125

photographer, 11, 21, 28, 45, 91, 107

piano, 46, 62, 115

pikeminnow, Colorado, 79

pioneer, 23, 24, 45, 52, 62, 79, 113, 114

Pipe Creek, 86, 86

Plateau Point, 25, 25

Point Imperial,110

pool table, 47

portage, 33–35, 33

Pothound, 74–75, 75

Powell, Emma, 22; Major John Wesley, 20–22, 20, 21, 27, 51, 101, 104–105, 104

Powell, expedition, 51; Point, 27–28

prarie dog, 76, 76

princess, 68–69

prohibition, 52

prospecting, 27, 39, 63, 96

prospector, 19, 21, 27, 37, 51, 51, 52, 71, 79, 91, 105

quicksand, 16, 40

raft, 21, 42, 43, 50, 66, 96, 105, 109

Rampart Cave, 58, 62, 79

rappel, 37, 58

rattlesnake, 48, 48, 81, 82–83, 82

raven, 77–78, 77

Redwall, 28, 30, 67, 76, 78, 110

Renner, George, 84–85

rescue, 21, 25, 39, 40, 41, 42, 42, 79, 102

Rice, Virginia, 48

ringtail, 76

Roaring Springs, 117

Rocky Mountains, 115

Roosevelt, Teddy, 71, 75, 93

Rough Riders, 19, 37

Russell, Charles, 114

Rust, David, 19

Saddle Canyon, 94

Saddle Mountain, 31

Salt Lake City, 25

San Juan River, 98

scalp, 52, 55

Schmidt, Justin, 80

scorpion, 80, 81–82

Sea of Cortez, 33

Separation Canyon, 104

sewage, 78

sheep, 87–88

sheer wall, 34–35, 39, 58, 87

Sheer Wall Rapid, 35

Sinumo Creek, 32

Sinyella, Juan, 27

skeleton, 106–107

skull, 91, 106, 107

Skywalk, 92

sloth, 58, 62

Smalley, George, 27–28

Smithsonian Institution, 48, 96, 101

Snake Ceremony, 22

snow, 16, 28, 30–31, 31, 46, 67, 72, 84, 86, 88, 88, 89, 91, 95

Sockdolager Rapid, 34

South Rim, 12, 18–19, 24, 27, 37, 45, 46, 56, 57, 59, 62, 74, 78–79, 86, 88, 93, 94, 99, 110, 111, 113, 114, 114

Spanish explorers, 14–15, 14, 27

spelunker, 29, 103

Spicer, Wells, 102–103

squirrel, 76, 98

Stanton, expedition, 79; Robert Brewster, 90, 91

Steck, George, 111

Steel, John, 16

Stevens, Larry, 79, 81

Stone Creek, 77

Stone, Julius, 22–23

string tie, 56, *56*

suicide, 106

Supai, 41, 46, 49, *49*

sweat lodge, 57

swim, 19, 23, *23*, 29, 35, 48, 94

Tanner, Seth, 103; Trail, 82, 94

Tapeats, Creek, 58, 116; Sandstone, 115

tarantula, 81, *81*

Teapot Dome, 96

temperature, 30–31, 87, 88, 95

teratorn, Merriams, 78

Thomas Flyer, 25

Thomas, Royal V., 25, *25*

Thompson, Almon Harris, *21*, 22; Martha, 63

tipi, 84

Tiyo, 20–21

Toledo Eight-horse, 24, *24*

Tolfree, J.H., 19

Tonto Trail, 112

Topocoba Trai, 46

topographic map, 58

Toroweap, Overlook, 35, *38*, 54, *54*; Valley, 113

Tovar, Pedro de, 53

Tracy, Warren, 73

trapper, 15, 23, 106

travertine, *26*, 27, 119

triple-rig, 49, *50*

trout, 79

turkey, 73, *73*

Tuweep, 62

U.S. Fish and Wildlife Service, 54

U.S. Geological Survey, 56

UFO, 102

Unkar Rapid, 42

Ute, 21

Van Dyke, John, 17

Vaseys Paradise, 29, *30*

venom, 81, 82–83

Villa, Pancho, 105

Vishnu Schist, 115, 117

Vulcans Anvil, 69, *69*

Walters, Ken, 30–31, 113

Warner, Charles Dudley, 17

Washburn, Bradford, 58

waterfall, *26*, 27, 28, 30, *30*, 42, 110–111, *111*, 116, *116*

weather, 29, 30, 84–86, 88

White, Georgie, 49–50, *50*; James, 20–21

whitewater, 42, 49

Whittlesey, Charles, 56

Williams, Al, 30; Tony, 37

Wilson, Dave, 65, 67; Wayne, 99

Wisher, Bryan, 42–43

Woolley, Edwin D., 25

Woolsey, Butte, 52; King, 52

wrangler, 63, 64–65, 67, 73, 110

Wylie Way Camp, *70*

Yaki Point, 47

Yavapai, 52

Young, Brigham, 16

Yount, George, 16

Many of the illustrations in this book were found in the archives of Grand Canyon National Park's Museum Collection and Northern Arizona University's Cline Library Special Collections and Archives. Image identification information is noted here.

Grand Canyon National Park Museum Collection

www.nps.gov/grca/photosmultimedia/index.htm

PAGE	IMAGE NUMBER
7	GRCA 14718
17	GRCA 03613
18	GRCA 14717 (upper) and GRCA 21349
20	GRCA 04907 (upper) and GRCA 17231 (lower)
21	GRCA 17234
24	GRCA 00589 (upper) and GRCA 05122 (lower)
25	GRCA 05255 (upper)
28	GRCA 11343
29	GRCA 16681
32	GRCA 16517(left) and GRCA 09796 (right)
36	GRCA 31333
37	GRCA 06930
40	GRCA 12093
41	GRCA 02106
44-45	GRCA 16250
47	GRCA 10111 (upper) and GRCA 03775 (lower)
50	GRCA 04810a (upper)
51	GRCA 08805 (upper)
52	GRCA 29303 (box), GRCA 29242 (tract), GRCA 29366-368 (photos)
53	GRCA 200504-0120 (photo)
55	GRCA 16180
57	18207a (upper)
59	GRCA 15144 (upper left), GRCA 15162 (lower left), GRCA 15224 (right), and GRCA 05549 (bottom)
60	GRCA 17506
61	GRCA 31349 (upper) and GRCA 00825 (lower)
63	GRCA 08995a (left) and GRCA 06935 (right)
70	GRCA 05271(lower)
72	GRCA 05275 (lower)
75	GRCA 05285
86	GRCA 03185
88	GRCA 00450
90	GRCA 05578
92	GRCA 14821
96	GRCA 06630
99	GRCA 05543
102	GRCA 31347
104	GRCA 17262
113	GRCA 00667
114	GRCA 03633

Cline Library Special Collections and Archives

www.nau.edu/~cline/speccoll/

PAGE	IMAGE NUMBER
23	NAU.PH.96.4.118.17C and NAU.PH.96.4.118.5B (upper two) NAU.PH.97.34.46 (lower)
30	NAU.PH.2003.11.4.5.N4251
31	NAU.PH.2003.11.4.7.B1553
50	NAU.PH.2003.11.4.6.H3831
51	NAU.PH.99.48 (upper)
62	NAU.PH.99.3.3.12.61
106	NAU.PH.568.4035
107	NAU.PH.563.5386

AUTHOR SCOTT THYBONY

Scott Thybony has traveled throughout North America on assignments for major magazines, including *National Geographic*, *Smithsonian*, and *Outside*. At various times he has found himself eating such delicacies as raw caribou with Inuit hunters, hors d'oeuvres with World Cup ski champions, and Dutch oven beer biscuits with river runners. His stories are heard on National Public Radio, and the Wilderness Society chose him as "Voice of the Land" for Grand Canyon. Twice, the National Geographic Society has awarded him grants for Grand Canyon explorations. His first job below the rim was washing dishes at Phantom Ranch, followed by work on the Colorado River as a boatman and river ranger. Since then the pay has improved but not the view.